Christa Black

GOD LOVES UGLY

& love makes beautiful

STUDY GUIDE

Groups / Individuals

45 Days to Freedom

To the thousands of *God Loves Ugly* readers
who kept asking me for more. Your hunger for
deeper freedom pulled these pages out of my heart,
so with love, this journey is for you.

CONTENTS

a note from
Christa

When I wrote *God Loves Ugly* in 2010, I didn't just write it for Christians. I wrote it for anyone who had experienced a broken heart.

At the time, my audience was a few million girls, giddily screaming at *The Jonas Brothers* who I just happened to be on stage with every night. And because I was within arms reach of their beloved Joe, Nick, and Kevin, thousands of those same girls (and a few brave fellows) followed my every move, and read every word I wrote. The last thing I wanted to do was to drive away the hurting because I wrote in a language they didn't understand called 'Christianese.'

I simply wanted to introduce them to this person who had what they were looking for—*Love*.

As time passed and I transitioned from a touring musician to an author and speaker, I realized very quickly how impossible it was for me to stand in front of a group of people and not gush about my Jesus. In fact, every time I opened my mouth, I didn't just speak—I preached.

To this day, I can't stop gushing about my Jesus. I can't stop opening my mouth and screaming from the rooftops about this God who made His home inside my heart for the purpose of healing it, restoring it, and linking me to His eternal love through intimacy.

This Study Guide is the result of that gushing. It's an overflow of what's already inside of me, filled with scripture, Jesus, God, the Holy Spirit, and everything in between. It's simply who I am.

But don't worry, friend. Even if Christianese is a foreign language to you, I know this God—this perfect Love—can still speak to your heart, taking the ugly places of our lives and making them beautiful. This Love continues to lead me into deeper waters of healing every day, and I know, if you'll let Him, He'll do the same for you.

xx,

Christa Black

HOW TO USE THIS STUDY GUIDE

GRAB YOUR COPY OF THE BOOK, *GOD LOVES UGLY*

The *God Loves Ugly Study Guide* was written to be used in conjunction with the book *God Loves Ugly*. Each lesson will include small readings from the book to prepare you to answer questions each day. Make sure and have your book handy and complete the assigned readings, otherwise, the lessons won't make much sense!

HOW LONG IS THIS STUDY?

This study includes 45 lessons to be completed over a 9-week period, either in groups or as individuals. Each week contains 5 lessons filled with devotionals, scriptures, and deeper insights from the chapters.

GLU GROUPS

If you've decided to lock arms with some friends and start a GLU GROUP (**G**od **L**oves **U**gly GROUP), then get ready for a roller coaster ride towards deep freedom and intimacy!

• **Facilitator:** Groups wander aimlessly without someone assigned to help direct them towards the Promised Land. Each group should assign a facilitator to help keep time, initiate prayer, and read questions, prompting participants to respond and making sure everyone has a chance to speak.

• **Assignments:** To make sure that you're ready to participate and get the most out of each meeting, read the assigned chapter in *God Loves Ugly* and complete the corresponding 5 lessons prior to your group each week.

• **Group Discussion Questions:** Turn to the discussion questions at the end of each chapter to begin your GLU GROUP, but remember, the listed questions are suggestions and not absolute requirements. Naturally navigate where the conversation is headed with the Holy Spirit's guidance. If God is moving while the group is discussing some hard heart-topics, then stay on that point and let Him work.

• **Time:** As women, we like to talk. But make sure that in a busy world where time is our most precious commodity, you put a time limit on your gathering and stick to it as much as possible.

BEFORE YOU GET STARTED

"As iron sharpens iron, so one man sharpens another." Proverbs 27:17

Freedom always costs something. There are many, however, who want it to be free.

When the Israelites crossed the threshold of the Promised Land, they didn't march in from the wilderness and politely ask the giants to leave. They took out their swords and prepared for battle. In order to occupy and live in their inheritance of freedom, they had to go to war.

You have an inheritance of freedom. The question is, are you willing to fight for it?

Most people are already at war, even if they don't know it—war for peace, wholeness and truth. But many stay on the defense, attempting to dodge disaster and survive past pain instead of charging forward and taking back what's been stolen. The problem is, you never learn to advance.

And, dear friend, you were created to advance from glory to glory.

As strong and amazing as I'm sure you are on your own, you can't take on armies of giants by yourself. There's a reason why God created us for relationship. We need one another. You need the people around you just as much as they need you. You need their wisdom and they need your experience. You need their strength and they need your vulnerability.

Lock arms and commit to taking on the giants inside your hearts together.

Accountability is powerful. Encouragement is necessary. And love is essential.

When armies arise together in unity, watch out world.

GLU GROUP REMINDERS

① THE NO-SHAME FLY ZONE

God has no shame or condemnation towards you (Romans 8:1), so why would you possibly have it towards yourself or towards one another? Remember this as people share things that are less than perfect. You will never understand someone's behaviors until you walk in their shoes, so commit to having greater grace, and declare a 'No-Shame Fly Zone' over your group.

② YOU'RE HERE FOR YOU

You're not here to be a counselor—you're here to find freedom for yourself. This isn't the time for you to have all the answers, appear to have it all together, and be the most spiritual. It's time for you to be painfully vulnerable. If you're concentrating on someone else's problem or diverting the attention from yourself, you will miss what God is trying to do in your own heart. Lean in and listen to what He wants to do for you. He has more for you than you can possibly imagine.

③ GET TO THE POINT

By all means, speak up, but remember to be concise and respectful of your time together. Engage in the group without dominating the conversation, and realize that each person deserves to have the platform.

④ CONFIDENTIALITY PACT

Whether you know each other well or are just acquaintances, everyone must feel safe in order to open up vaulted areas of the heart. Understand the importance of total confidentiality while things come to the surface. Make a verbal commitment to one another, to the process of healing, and to love and respect each other by keeping your lips sealed!

week one
God Loves Ugly **Introduction**

Day 1: **THE DOCTOR IS IN**

Read 'War for Peace,' page xi in *God Loves Ugly*.

Imagine yourself sitting alone on a doctor's examining table waiting for the results of a few recent tests.

You fidget nervously, swinging your feet back and forth as they dangle down, trying to act as natural as possible while your heart beats so loudly, you swear someone is going to run in and tell you to quiet down. Over the course of your life, you've become a master at managing pain—always finding ways to numb it, hide it, or simply ignore it. But the shooting pain inside your heart has grown increasingly strong with time—too strong to keep ignoring, despite your best efforts. You long to know the results from your latest medical tests, in fact, you haven't slept for a week imagining every morbid possibility. But deep down, you're petrified of really knowing the truth.

What if there is something terribly wrong with you?
What if your heart fails you?
Even worse, what if you might die?

The doctor enters the room wearing his white coat and warm smile, casually holding a bright yellow folder with your name written in large black letters. You want to yell at him to hold onto the test results as though your life depended on it, but you hold your tongue, along with your breath.

"Well, my friend," he says as he scoots his stool uncomfortably close, his gaze concerned but inviting. "I'm afraid I have some bad news."

With every word of his wrecking ball diagnosis, your body numbs. Did he really just say you're dying? How could this be true? His words hit your soul like a head-on collision. It's apparently going to be a slow process, and a painful one, too. And the disease that began in your **heart** has made it's way into your **head**, now **slowly attacking the rest of your body**. If you continue living the way you're living, eventually, it will kill you.

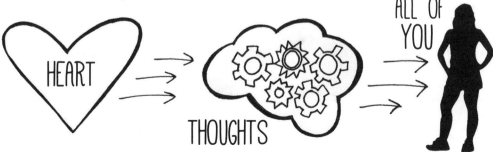

"BUT," he says with a confident smile, "There's hope."

You lean in close, clinging to his every word. If you do what this doctor says, following his expertise, and making a few changes while diligently and intentionally sticking to the program, a miracle can happen.

Your heart will be healed.

And you won't just survive...

you'll come alive.

After leaving the doctor's office, what do you do? Do you follow His expert advice, or do you ignore him and keep living the way you've been living?

_____

_____

_____

Unless you're a walking corpse with a death wish, it's a pretty safe bet you're going to start the process of eliminating your heart disease, immediately implementing whatever plan the doctor prescribed. If he told you to stand on your head every day and recite the words "I am healed" until you toppled over, you better believe you'd do it. If he told you a new study proved that drinking goats milk and wheatgrass did the trick, you'd tip up that cup in a heartbeat. Maybe he prescribed dipping in the local river seven times, and as ludicrous as it may seem, I have a hunch you'd at least try it. People do crazy things when they're desperate for healing.

But why wait until you're desperate?

Be honest with yourself for a moment. What are you willing to do in order to heal from the brokenness inside your heart?

_____

_____

_____

Maybe you're already desperate. Will you commit to doing whatever the doctor tells you to do?

_____

_____

_____

Many people aren't aware they need heart-healing. As long as they can manage the pain, they just keep on keeping on. For years, I wasn't aware that numbing pain with substances was an indication that I needed to heal—until it turned into unmanageable addictions. Because I was rail thin, I never saw my secret bingeing as a problem—until I started gaining weight and ended up in rehab for an eating disorder. I never saw getting wasted on the weekend as an issue—until one night I ended up with a guy on top of me, taking what wasn't his to take. I never saw my internal anger as a problem—until one day when I blew a fuse, I started throwing punches.

Some of you don't have heart-pain that has manifested quite as obviously as mine did. Maybe you had a great family and a solid upbringing, so you don't see your insecurity as a major problem. Maybe you've always been a bit fearful, or a worrier, or anxious, so you believe this is the way life has to be. But self-hatred is a problem. Depression is a problem. Hopelessness is a problem. Bitterness, jealousy, unforgiveness, anger, perfectionism—these are all indicators that your heart needs a Healer.

Close your eyes, take a few minutes and ask the Holy Spirit to search deep inside. Is there pain inside your heart that you might not be aware of? Write out the words, pictures, memories, or feelings that you experience.

Have you tried to hide, numb, medicate, or run from this pain? Take a minute and write down all the ways you've tried to medicate the pain.

_____

_____

_____

Is this pain affecting your relationships? Your job? Your marriage and children? Your health, weight, or appearance? Explain below.

_____

_____

_____

You weren't created to live in constant pain. You were created to live from a whole heart, healed from the brokenness of this life. Good news—the Doctor is in. There's a concrete promise in the Bible that when you go through painful experiences in this world, there is One who will walk with you, bringing peace.

"These things I have spoken to you, so that in Me you may have peace. In the world you have tribulation, but take courage; I have overcome the world." John 16:33 (NAS)

What does this promise mean to you?

_____

_____

If this promise is hard to believe, tell God about it right now. Tell Him how you don't trust Him. Tell Him how you're angry at Him. Tell Him how you feel hopeless. Whatever you feel—get it out in the open where you're not carrying the load on your own. He can handle it—I promise—and He's not angry at you. He just needs you to be honest.

_____

_____

_____

_____

_____

_____

Thank you, Jesus our Healer, for this journey of heart healing. You came that we might be whole. You came that we might have life, and have it abundantly. Protect and guard every heart in the days and weeks to come—that the fullness of life would come in and heal every heart! Amen.

Day 2: OUCH, LIFE. YOU HURT.

Over the course of my colorful life, I've noticed a consistent fact about humanity. At some point, every one of us has been broken by the pain of life, and this pain can end up dictating the tone of our existence on this earth. When our hearts aren't healed properly from the wounds of the past, our present/future pays the price.

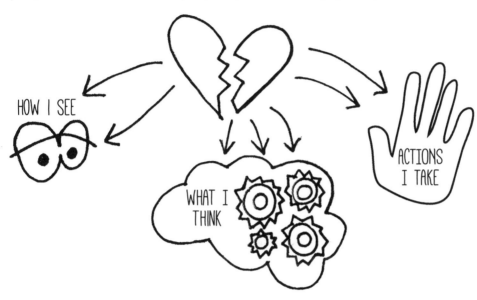

I don't know about you, but managing pain every day sounds like an awful existence on this earth to me. Especially since we have access to a Doctor who heals every wound. It's time for our hearts to be healed so our lives can be abundant.

In John 10:10, Jesus says, "I came so they can have real and eternal life, more and better life than they ever dreamed of." (MSG)

In this verse, do you think that Jesus is talking about having a better life someday when death comes? Or is He talking about right now, as you're breathing on this earth?

_____

_____

_____

Now the Lord is the Spirit, and where
the Spirit of the Lord is, there is liberty
(emancipation from bondage, freedom).
2 Corinthians 3:17 (Amplified)

This Jesus came that we might have the fullness of life **right now.** That means you can be totally free from your insecurity. That means you can be free from your eating disorder. It means you don't have to manage your addiction, depression, or trauma from the past. It means that there's a solution for your weight issue. It means your marriage isn't a lost cause. It means that there's freedom from your toxic thoughts, your obsessions with your body, your cutting, and the battle that goes on every time you look at yourself in the mirror.

But it starts with the healing of your broken heart.

Take a minute to think about abundant life. What would this kind of life look like to you? And be specific. (finances, relationships, children, health, job, etc.)

_____

_____

_____

What would need to be eliminated in order for you to have abundant life?

_____

_____

_____

What would need to be added in order for you to have abundant life?

_____

_____

_____

> *"So if the Son liberates you [makes you free men], then you are really and unquestionably free." John 8:36* (Amplified)

Does this promise seem impossible? Do you believe there are certain parts of your life that will never be completely free until you die? Maybe you've always been fearful, insecure, shy, angry, manipulative, jealous, or addicted.

Do you believe you can never really change? If so, be honest and write down your thoughts.

_____

_____

_____

Beautiful friend, the Doctor has your test results in His hand _and_ **He's not worried**. He has so much faith in Himself as a Doctor. He's absolutely certain that He can fix every problem because He knows way more about your heart than you do. Yes, there are things that will need to change, but He'll let you know exactly what to do, and you get to partner with Him in the process. Yes, you might need to have surgery and let Him open you up and go inside, but He's masterfully skilled and has never lost a patient. If you listen to this Doctor's diagnosis of your heart, letting Him examine what's deep within, He's going to heal you and make you whole.

If you're up for living life to the fullest, free from the brokenness of your past, your shame, your trauma, and your current bondage, then commit right now to this process of heart-healing. If the Doctor sends you home with a medication, He's not going to be looking over your shoulder making sure you take your meds.

It's up to you.

You have the choice, right now, to let the Doctor inside your heart and prescribe a path towards total healing. And then you have a choice whether or not to walk it out.

Will you let the Doctor examine your heart in the days and weeks ahead? Just like a doctor needs written consent to perform certain medical procedures, give God your consent to go ahead with His heart examination. Write out your written consent below.

_____

_____

_____

Now that you've given Him consent to go inside, write out your commitment to implementing these changes to help you walk into heart-wholeness?

_____

_____

_____

Day 3: THE PRESCRIPTION

Read **Isaiah 61:1-7** today, letting the promises soak in deep, amping you up for the journey ahead. This passage was a foretelling of the primary purpose of Jesus as He came to earth—to heal the brokenness of mankind, restoring us to relationship with the Father.

> *The Spirit of God, the Master, is on me*
> *because God anointed me.*
> *He sent me to preach good news to the poor,*
> *heal the heartbroken,*

What would it feel like for your broken heart to be completely healed?

_____

_____

_____

> *Announce freedom to all captives,*
> *pardon all prisoners.*

Meditate on total freedom for a moment. You might have partial freedom right now, but that's not good enough. What would total freedom look like?

_____

_____

_____

> *God sent me to announce the year of his grace—*
> *a celebration of God's destruction of our enemies—*
> *and to comfort all who mourn...*

Are there enemies in your life that need destroying? Do you need comforting?

_____

_____

To care for the needs of all who mourn in Zion,
give them bouquets of roses instead of ashes,
Messages of joy instead of news of doom,
a praising heart instead of a languid spirit.

Do you have needs that need caring for? What about life being birthed from the ashes of your past? Could you use a dose of joy instead of despair?

_____

_____

_____

Rename them "Oaks of Righteousness"
planted by God to display his glory.

Think about an oak for a moment, on display for the world to see. It says that God plants this oak, not that you have to become one. Are there things you believed you needed to become for God? What if He's the only One who can make you into the strong, beautiful tree you're created to be?

_____

_____

_____

They'll rebuild the old ruins,
raise a new city out of the wreckage.
They'll start over on the ruined cities,
take the rubble left behind and make it new.

What would it look like for God to take the old ruins of your past, making them beautiful and new?

_____

_____

_____

You'll hire outsiders to herd your flocks
and foreigners to work your fields,
But you'll have the title "Priests of God,"
honored as ministers of our God.
You'll feast on the bounty of nations,
you'll bask in their glory.

Imagine having so much abundance in your life, you'll need help managing that amount of blessing. Take a few minutes to meditate on a surplus of abundance in your life. What would that look like?

_____

_____

_____

Because you got a double dose of trouble
and more than your share of contempt,
Your inheritance in the land will be doubled
and your joy go on forever. (NASB)

God makes a promise here to the broken. Every bit of trouble that has come at you, He'll take that trouble and double your inheritance, giving you joy forever—starting NOW.

What trouble have you had so far?

_____

_____

_____

Now, here's the exciting part. Take all that trouble, and double a blessing back on your life. What would it look like for the things that have been stolen to be repaid double?

_____

_____

_____

_____

Day 4: **WALKING IT OUT**

There once was a girl stuck in a flood.

As the waters rose inside her home, she climbed high on top of her roof to escape, praying to God for rescue. Being an avid Bible-reader and regular churchgoer, she sat confidently in the rain as the storm raged, knowing the promises of God for rescue and salvation.

An old man in a boat came by, screaming at her to jump in. The girl examined the old fishing boat, paint chipping from worn wood that had seen years in rough waters, the smell of fish still strong, even in the wind. Surely this wasn't the way God had planned to rescue her. The man was so frail and decrepit, and his boat was so dirty and rickety. Not to mention the foul smell.

"No, that's okay," she replied with a smile. "My God has promised to rescue me, and I'm just waiting for Him to show up."

Baffled and confused, the old man paddled away to safety as the water continued to rise.

Shortly thereafter, a rescue helicopter flew overhead looking for people in trouble. With bullhorn in hand, the rescuer yelled down to the girl, "Don't worry, ma'am—we're here to save you from the floods! Now, stand up and we'll throw you a ladder!"

Strangely enough, the girl stayed seated. The rope ladder seemed dangerous as it swayed violently in the wind. Surely God wouldn't ask her to risk her life to be rescued, or do something that might take that much effort. She was already exhausted from climbing up onto the roof, and how much more energy would she have to exert to climb that ladder as the wind howled. She shooed the helicopter away while shaking her head back and forth, "That's okay," she screamed. "I appreciate it, but I'm just waiting on God. He's promised to rescue me!"

With many people yet to save and no time to argue, the helicopter quickly flew away.

The waters continued to rise as the rain fell from the heavens—rising up above the girl's head. With nothing left to hold onto and her strength growing weak, she finally surrendered and sank beneath the waters, breathing out her last breath on this earth.

When the girl got to heaven, she had some questions for this God who had promised to save her. She had been so faithful to His promises, which is what she thought He wanted. She had been so confident in His word, sitting down and waiting for Him as the storm raged. Hadn't she done everything right? Hadn't she been a faith-filled Bible believing girl, and hadn't her actions proved that?

"God, why didn't you save me like You promised," she asked with tears in her eyes.

"My dear daughter," replied the Father, compassionately scooping up His little girl, holding her close. "I tried."

She looked up at him, confused.

"I sent a boat, but you didn't get in. Then I sent you a helicopter, but you refused to climb the ladder. They didn't meet *your* standards, but they met mine. You wanted me to rescue you in a certain way that required little to no effort on your part—you didn't want to get dirty or soiled in the process. But my only goal was to see you saved."

How many times have we missed our rescue because it didn't look like we wanted it to look? Or, because we didn't do everything we could to climb to freedom?

Take a minute and think about this story and how it relates to your own life. Are there scriptures you know God has given you that you haven't let transform your heart? Have there been things you've held onto (bitterness, unforgiveness, anger, shame, pain) that you know are poisoning your soul?

Most times, we want to be free but we haven't done everything we can in order to get there. We want the Promised Land, but we don't want to fight giants.

Have you wanted a magic pill that would take all the pain away? Have you wanted to wake up instantly different, not doing your part to walk into freedom?

_____

_____

_____

What are you willing to do to walk into the land of freedom God has promised all of His kids? What are you willing to give up and change in order to live in this land?

_____

_____

_____

_____

_____

Day 5: **THE COMMODITY OF TIME**

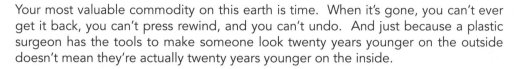

Your most valuable commodity on this earth is time. When it's gone, you can't ever get it back, you can't press rewind, and you can't undo. And just because a plastic surgeon has the tools to make someone look twenty years younger on the outside doesn't mean they're actually twenty years younger on the inside.

Time ticks on whether we want it to or not.

One of the main excuses I hear when asking people to make life-changes towards freedom is, *"Christa, I just don't have enough time."*

Well, let's put that theory to the test. For the next 3 days, lets see just how much time you have, and just how much time you waste. Let's see how much time you're spending on things that are bringing death, and how much time you're spending on things that bring you life.

If you know that you're a worrier, I want you to clock the amount of time you worry. If you know you're fearful and insecure, see how much of your time real-estate you give to building that kind of property in your head and heart. How much time do you spend hanging out with Jesus? How much time do you spend checking out in front of the television? How much time do you spend getting ready? How much time do you spend cooking, cleaning, taking care of kids, sleeping?

And the big one...

How much time do you spend on your smartphone or computer checking, refreshing, and updating social media sites?

No shame here. Let's just get an overall picture of how much time you really have, and how much time you have to apply towards freedom.

DAY 1	DAY 2	DAY 3
_____	_____	_____
_____	_____	_____
_____	_____	_____
_____	_____	_____
_____	_____	_____
_____	_____	_____
_____	_____	_____

Week 1: GROUP DISCUSSION QUESTIONS

1 Read *War for Peace* (xi) and *August 1999* (page 1) aloud.

2 **Begin with a prayer, asking God to safely cover hearts as they begin to open up and heal.** Declare Psalm 91 over your time. "Whoever dwells in the shelter of the Most High will rest in the shadow of the Almighty." (NIV) That He will "cover you with His feathers, and under His wings will you find refuge."

3 **Discussion Questions:**
• After reading *War for Peace*, have there been things that you've tried in the past that didn't work before—maybe a book, seminar, conference, counseling, church, or group study? Is there any fear that this won't work and that nothing will change? If so, are you still harboring disappointment?

• For those of you who answered yes, discuss John 8:36. *"If the Son has set you free, you are free indeed."* According to that verse, what would freedom look like in your own life? Have you set your expectations for freedom on your past experience, or on what God has said?

• Bondage can take on many forms. Fear, anxiety, self-hatred, bitterness, people pleasing, and insecurity are bondage for the human soul just as much as eating disorders, addictions, sexual dysfunction, and cutting are to the body. Is there anything that you've lived with for so long, you truly believe that you can never change?

• Have someone takes notes on this question as the group discusses, writing down the things about your lives that you want to change, but believe never will. Hang onto this list and put it somewhere safe until the end of week 10.

• For those willing to share their answers with the group, write down a group sheet titled **'We Believe God Can.'** Bring this list every week and read it aloud at the beginning of the group.

4 **Close with a prayer, declaring that God will fulfill His promise of freedom for every heart.**

5 **Have *Chapter 1* and the assignments completed by the next time you meet. (Pages 2-24)**

week two
Chapter 1 The Love Bucket

Day 1: **THE LOVE BUCKET**

Read pages 5-20 in *God Loves Ugly*.

No matter what your culture, religion, or country of origin, every person on the planet wants, needs, and longs for one main thing: **LOVE**. In fact, your heart is simply a big bucket made for the stuff! That's how genius our God is—when we say yes to Jesus, **Love** comes and makes His home inside of us.

The solution for every problem you've ever faced already lives inside of you!

The problem is, we've all been punched by life at some point—while we were Christians or not. And if we don't allow the Healer to bind up our broken hearts, our buckets stay holey, in the wrong sense of the word.

1. What's inside the love bucket of your heart? Are you filled with love, or self-criticism? Maybe jealousy, bitterness, unforgiveness? Are you filled with anger or kindness, worry or peace? Write down all the things that have your permission to reside inside of your love bucket.

2. Everyone has found themselves with a hole punched in their love bucket at some point, but not everyone has allowed those punches to be healed and patched up. Draw the places, relationships, and circumstances where life may have punched you and you've found it hard to mend.

3. Do you want your love bucket to be filled, but deep down, you don't think you're worthy of love? Do you try to earn love or approval with performance, perfectionism, and achievement? If it's hard for you to receive love, encouragement, gifts, or praises because of shame or inadequacy, draw a barrier over the top of your bucket.

Write or draw your answers for questions 1-3 in the bucket to the right.

4. Now that your bucket is filled up and you've identified certain 'holes' punched in your heart from pain, examine the bucket of your heart. Does it feel like there's more pain in there than peace? More hurt than love? Or maybe the areas of pain are small, but they seem to require a lot of attention? Write your observations below.

_____

_____

_____

_____

_____

_____

_____

Pain is a hungry monster, always needing to be fed. Our hearts weren't created to be in constant pain, especially since the monster of pain always screams to be numbed, silenced, or covered up.

Go back to your bucket and write out any ways you might numb, medicate, silence, cover up, or try to hide pain inside your love bucket. (*Example: eating disorders; escapism; obsession with body, children, or substances; addictions; depression; seclusion; television; Internet; business; serving*)

Thank you, Jesus, that you know our hearts better than we do. Thank you that you're not overwhelmed by what's inside our hearts, so we take a deep breath, and sink deep into your arms of love. We trust you in the days and weeks ahead to heal our brokenness as we partner with your truth. Amen.

Day 2: **THE LIST**

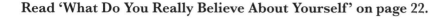

Read 'What Do You Really Believe About Yourself' on page 22.

It's sometimes easy to pull out our magnifying glass and examine others—especially those who have hurt us. We examine the blemishes, the problems and the faults with an eagle eye, having opinions and judgments about everyone and everything. But turning that same magnifying glass on ourselves can sometimes be painful, especially in the heart department.

> *"A presumed knowledge of that which is right or wrong does not qualify you to judge anyone. Especially if you do exactly the same stuff you notice other people do wrong. You effectively condemn yourself. No man is another man's judge."*
> ***Romans 2:1*** (The Mirror Bible)

Meditate on the words of the apostle Paul for a moment, lowering our magnifying glass aimed at others. **Do you find it easy to judge others, essentially condemning yourself?**

_____

_____

_____

Proverbs 23:7 says *"For as he thinks in his heart, so is he."* (AKJV)

Let the weight of that scripture sink in for a minute. **You are what you believe you are inside of your heart.** You act that way. You think that way. You speak that way.

Proverbs 4:23 *"Guard your heart above all else, for it determines the course of your life."* (NLT)

If what's inside your heart determines the course of your life, then don't you think it might be important to find out what's going on in there? Before you started this study, did you even have a clue or give much thought as to what was inside your heart?

_____

_____

_____

Stop for a second and ask the Holy Spirit, who leads us into all truth, to hold up *His* magnifying glass. (John 16:13) It's never wise to go soul-searching without His light shining. You'll just get depressed and overwhelmed, which is not the way He works. When God reveals a part of your heart that needs to heal, He's just pointing with excitement to what He's about to heal next! And believe me, there's nothing too impossible about your pain that He hasn't already taken care of at the cross.

Take ten minutes, get quiet and listen, letting Him lead you deep inside the corridors of your heart. What's going on in there? **What do you really believe about yourself? And where did those beliefs come from?**

Write out the most important list of your life, etched permanently on the outside of your love bucket. Because this list determines who you are.

Thank you, Holy Spirit, for showing me what I believe about myself. I know some of my beliefs don't line up with what you believe about me, and I'm ready for truth to be revealed, washing me clean, transforming my heart, and setting me free! Amen.

Day 3: **HEADSPACE**

Read 'What Thoughts Consistently Roll Through Your Head' on page 22.

Up until this point, you've learned how all of your experiences, good or bad, determined the condition of your love bucket. Maybe you haven't had major wounds in your life, but you still feel stuck and you can't figure out why. Remember, it only takes one hole to drain a bucket.

Take a moment and write out any wounds that have punched permanent holes in your love bucket. (Examples: abuse, rape, divorce, loss, bullying, abandonment, etc)

_____

_____

_____

Has your love bucket been wounded because you didn't get what you needed through nurture, acceptance, affection, and love?

_____

_____

_____

If the places of woundedness and pain inside our hearts aren't allowed to heal properly, they affect every part of our lives. ***Especially our thinking.***

Have you paid much attention to your thinking, both conscious and subconscious? Write out the thoughts that you know you've already had about yourself today, both positive and negative. (Hint: you probably had a lot of them while getting ready in front of the mirror this morning!)

What are repetitive thoughts that you have about yourself on an almost daily basis? They could be about your physical body, or maybe your personality. Do you have thoughts about how much you have, or how much you're lacking? Does your thinking tend to be more positive or negative? Write out the patterns that you see below.

If our thinking has a tendency to lean toward the negative, it makes sense in 2 Corinthians 10:5 that Paul would urge us to take care of our thoughts: *"casting down imaginations, and every high thing that is exalted against the knowledge of God, and bringing every thought into captivity to the obedience of Christ;"* (ASV)

Take a minute and think about how you use your imagination. When you were a child, your imagination was used for all sorts of amazing adventures. But the older we get, a lot of times our imaginations are used to try and figure out what's going to happen in the future, leading to all sorts of worries, fears, and 'how in the world is that going to pan out' emotions. In the words of my pastor Bill Johnson, *"Any thought you have about the future without the Holy Spirit is subject to distortion."*

How much time do you spend thinking about the future, potentially causing anxiety, fear, and worry over things you can't control?

_____

_____

_____

_____

_____

What would it look like for you to take your thoughts captive and stop future-tripping inside of your mind, imagining all sorts of outcomes and scenarios that aren't guaranteed? Would you have to be on the lookout for certain thought-

patterns that cause toxic thinking? No war is won without a strategy of attack. Write out your strategy for taking certain toxic thoughts captive.

_____

_____

_____

How much time do you spend thinking about your past and all the things you can never change? Does this type of thinking bring feelings of shame and regret, inadequacy and insecurity, or healing and wholeness?

_____

_____

_____

God makes it very clear—it's up to *us* to wrangle our thoughts to the ground. You're the only one who holds the keys to the real estate of your head, allowing thoughts to roam free through the gate of choice.

Dr. Caroline Leaf teaches in her books *Who Switched Off My Brain* and *Switch on Your Brain* that 75% to 95% of the illnesses that plague our bodies today are a direct result of our negative thought life. What we think about affects us both physically and emotionally. And research has found that fear triggers more than 1,400 known physical and chemical responses, activating more than thirty different hormones.

If negative thinking is aiding the destruction of your life, both physically and emotionally, take a minute and write out a prayer, asking God to help you recognize the thinking that doesn't line up with the truth. Ask Him to help you take those thoughts captive and kick them out of your head...

Permanently.

_____

_____

_____

_____

_____

_____

Day 4: DECLARATIONS

Read 'Declarations' on pages 23-24.

Words are far more powerful than you might have imagined, for they hold the power of creation.

In Genesis when God created the earth, He didn't clap His hands or throw a lightning rod. *He spoke.* He opened His mouth and everything that you see was created. Words create something inside of our hearts that either grows and blooms with life, or poisons to kill your soul.

Have you given much thought to the power of your words? Do you see how the words spoken to you and by you have created either healing or pain? Write out your thoughts below.

_____

_____

_____

"So faith comes from hearing, and hearing through the word of Christ." Romans 10:17 (ESV)

The reason why it's far more important for you to *speak* the truth over your life, rather than simply reading and thinking it, is because you need to **hear** in order to **believe**. Your spoken word actually creates something in your heart. It creates faith.

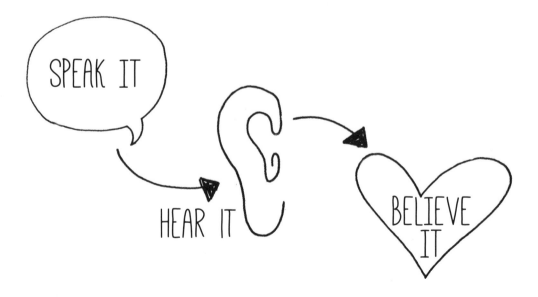

And what is faith?

> *"Now faith is the substance of things hoped for, the evidence of things not seen." Hebrews 11:1* (KJV)

Faith is a substance. It's not a theory or an invisible feeling. It brings about the substance all our hearts have hoped for.

It's time to begin challenging the beliefs, thoughts, and words that have defined your life up until this point—especially if those beliefs, thoughts, and words are creating destruction in your soul.

Go back to pages 28-30, compiling two lists:
> **1. What do you believe about yourself?**
> **2. What do you think about yourself?**

If you're anything like me, your negative list might have been far longer than your positive one. Overall, my life had way more positives than negatives, but the few bad things that had happened kept overriding the good, destroying everything.

Think about a baby rattle snake for a moment. Isn't it crazy how one little bite from a creature that's a fraction of the size of a human, if left untreated, can kill parts of your body, possibly even causing death?

Take your negative lists, and begin to challenge those negatives in the form of declarations:

"I challenge the core belief that I am _____ and do not accept this belief in my mind and heart anymore. I'm choosing today to believe that I am_____, regardless of what I see or feel."

For instance, one of my core beliefs was that I would never have true intimacy because of the imperfections in my body. I believed that my cellulite would cause future love interests to be so disappointed, they wouldn't end up wanting me. Years ago when I began to challenge that belief, I wrote these words in my journal:

"I challenge the core belief that I am <u>unlovable if I don't have a perfect body</u> and do not accept this belief in my mind and heart anymore. I'm choosing today to believe that I am <u>worthy of being loved AS I AM,</u> regardless of what I see or feel."

Did I instantly believe this truth in my heart after saying it once? Not a chance. But I took the first step in clearing the black fog over my head. There's more work to be done in the days and weeks ahead, but you're taking the first steps to clear the air to see clearly.

Take your time to work through this list, crafting your words below. Make sure every negative is challenged and the truth is fought to be uncovered.

After you've completed this assignment, go somewhere alone in front of a mirror and *speak* this list **OUT LOUD** where your ears, mind, and heart can hear it. You might feel crazy, but do it anyway. It might be difficult to make eye contact with the one you despise so deeply. But change doesn't happen on its own, especially after years of programming.

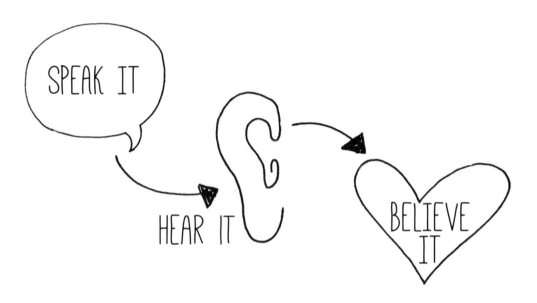

Pick up this sword, the words of your mouth, and begin to declare your freedom.
(this will be a long list)

_____

_____

_____

_____

_____

_____

_____

_____

Day 5: TILLING THE SOIL

SEEDS OF TRUTH

Last week, my dad began his springtime ritual of planting all sorts of vegetables in his back-yard garden. And because dirt was involved, my two-year-old son Moses was eager to help. With gardening shovels in hand, they began tilling the hardened soil, preparing the land to receive the seeds of life.

The declarations of your mouth till the hardened soil inside your heart.

The truth of these words plant seeds deep inside.

But unfortunately, this alone doesn't ensure growth. It's just the first step. You're still going to need water and sunlight to bring forth the harvest of life.

I wish that telling you to stand in front of a mirror and daily speak the words, "I am beautiful" had magical powers to make you actually believe you're beautiful. The problem is, you might have had years of experiences that proved the opposite to be true. And enough painful experiences end up wounding your heart. Your new declarations of truth will start clearing space in your head and heart for change, tilling the hardened soil of your heart, but there's more work to be done.

You need an experienced Gardener with powerful water and light to pour over the seeds, bringing forth life.

How did your new declarations make you feel as you spoke them aloud yesterday? Did you feel like an impostor? Did you feel like a liar? Did you feel empowered? Did you feel walls begin to come down in your heart? Could you even make eye contact with yourself? Write your observations below.

_____

_____

_____

_____

_____

In order for you to see life produced in your heart, you've got to keep the soil softened with the truth, and make sure the seed doesn't get snatched or choked away.

Read the parable of the Harvest in Matthew 13:3-8

"What do you make of this? A farmer planted seed. As he scattered the seed, some of it fell on the road, and birds ate it. Some fell in the gravel; it sprouted quickly but didn't put down roots, so when the sun came up it withered just as quickly. Some fell in the weeds; as it came up, it was strangled by the weeds. Some fell on good earth, and produced a harvest beyond his wildest dreams." (MSG)

Have you ever thought about the soil of your heart? We all want life to spring up from the inside, but we might not know how to get seeds to grow with rocks, gravel, and weeds still inside.

Your commitment to declaring the truth into the soil of your heart is your promise to keep the seed inside. If you're willing to keep this new truth inside your heart, make a commitment below to verbally declare your new list in front of your mirror *every day for the next forty days.*

I, _____, commit to declaring the truth into my life, keeping the seed of the word of truth in the soil of my heart. I commit to doing this every day, at least once a day, for forty days.

Let's read further in Matthew 13:18-23

"Study this story of the farmer planting seed. When anyone hears news of the kingdom and doesn't take it in, it just remains on the surface, and so the Evil One comes along and plucks it right out of that person's heart. This is the seed the farmer scatters on the road.

"The seed cast in the gravel—this is the person who hears and instantly responds with enthusiasm. But there is no soil of character, and so when the emotions wear off and some difficulty arrives, there is nothing to show for it.

"The seed cast in the weeds is the person who hears the kingdom news, but weeds of worry and illusions about getting more and wanting everything under the sun strangle what was heard, and nothing comes of it.

"The seed cast on good earth is the person who hears and takes in the News, and then produces a harvest beyond his wildest dreams." (MSG)

After reading this parable, take a minute and assess the soil of your heart.

Do you feel like truth stays on the surface, being stolen away before it has a chance to grow life?

_____

_____

_____

Is the soil of your heart full of gravel? Maybe you've been excited in a church setting or after an encounter with God, but after the emotional high wears off, the truth never takes root, and change is never produced.

_____

_____

_____

Is your heart full of the weeds of worry and illusions? Do you hear the truth, but then your head takes over, and you talk yourself out of the truth so it's never allowed to produce life?

_____

_____

_____

Is the soil of your heart fertile ground, ready for the truth to take root, producing a supernatural harvest beyond your wildest dreams? If this is something you want, write out your longing for this heart-soil below.

_____

_____

_____

_____

_____

Your heart is your property. It's your land. You might not have been able to decide what rocks have come against your soil, what hail, what storms, what famine, and what weeds have grown up in the past. But right now, you have a choice to declare the truth, tilling up the hardened soil of your heart. And right now, you have a choice to keep the seeds of that truth from being stolen or choked away.

That is your goal over the next forty days. And I promise you, if you keep and guard these seeds of truth inside your heart, they will eventually produce a harvest. A harvest of inheritance.

A harvest beyond your wildest dreams.

Week 2: GROUP DISCUSSION QUESTIONS

Chapter 1: The Love Bucket

1 **Begin with a prayer, giving God permission to do whatever He needs to do.** Declare 2 Corinthians 3:17 over your group: "Now the Lord is the Spirit, and where the Spirit of the Lord is, there is freedom." (NASB)

2 **Read the 'We Believe God Can' list aloud.** Set your expectation on what God promises to do, not on what reality might have been. Briefly give any testimony of your declarations blooming to life over the past week.

3 **Discussion Questions:**
• You were created to be filled with the perfect love of God. In reading about the Love Bucket of your heart, what condition is your bucket in? Is it healed and complete, or does it seem to have holes from the wounds of your past that make it feel empty and broken?

• If your Love Bucket feels empty, what are some of the things you use to fill it? (Food, achievement, friends, alcohol, sex, exercise, ministry, business, kids, romance, Internet, TV, drugs, fantasy).

• We all look at God, ourselves, and the world through the lens of our beliefs. What were some of the main lies you believed about yourself that you weren't even conscious of? What experiences did those lies come from? Name one or two lies that were the hardest to discover.

• Changing your mind and heart doesn't happen overnight. Confess to the group one lie that still seems impossible to ever believe. Ask them for a scripture that reinforces the truth, speaking it aloud in the form of a declaration this next week.

• What are some of the dangers of perfectionism and performance? Why is hiding shame and weakness a hindrance to your freedom?

• You have two lists. Talk about what it felt like to declare the truth over your life. Was it difficult? Did it feel empowering?

• What did you discover about the soil of your heart? Do you believe you can keep the seeds of truth from being stolen or choked away for forty days?

4 **Close with a prayer, declaring that God will fulfill His promise of freedom for every heart.**

5 **Have *Chapter 2* and the assignments completed by the next time you meet. (Pages 26-43)**

week three
Chapter 2 Sticks and Stones

Day 1: **Goodness Amnesia**

Read pages 29-38 in *God Loves Ugly*.

My parents told me I was beautiful almost every day while I was growing up. But the strange thing is, I don't have any recollection of them saying it. *Ever.* It's as if a mean little monster crawled into my brain and blotted out every one of their beautiful words with a magic eraser. I can tell you, however, every time a boy told me I was ugly, or pointed to my 'pig nose,' or said I had a big butt, or called me a dog. I can tell you almost every time I was rejected, made fun of, sat alone at a school dance, or was excluded. Those memories seem carved in stone, unable to be jogged from my memory.

Isn't it interesting how we might have a lifetime of good words and experiences, and then one encounter with pain can occur and cause 'goodness amnesia?' It's kind of like a tiny paper cut, barely noticeable to the naked eye. Paper cuts are almost invisible, they don't usually bleed, and they're definitely not going to kill anybody. But man, that paper cut can sting. Before you know it, that tiny cut is so annoying it's all you can think about, forgetting that the rest of your body might be perfectly fine.

After reading *Chapter 2: Sticks & Stones*, have you realized you might have some 'goodness amnesia?' Have the painful words spoken against your life caused you to forget about the good and focus on the bad?

Take a few minutes and meditate on the good words that have been spoken about you over the years. They might have been from a praying grandmother, an empowering teacher, a mentor, or parents who adopted and loved on you. Maybe there was one friend who never let you down, or a sibling who stopped fighting with you long enough to be kind. What compliments does your spouse or friend try to give you that you keep brushing off? Write out at least five good things spoken over your life that you haven't focused on in a while.

1 _____

2 _____

_____

③ _____

_____

④ _____

_____

⑤ _____

_____

Many of the painful, abusive, and negative words spoken about us did a great job of slashing up our fragile hearts. And when those words aren't replaced and stay deep inside, we stay crippled with blurred vision.

Your eyes see through your heart.

Reality is never about your reflection—*it's about your perception.* Whatever you believe in your heart is what you're going to see in the mirror—no matter how perfect you look.

What do you see? When you look in the mirror do you see through the negative words that have been spoken about you, or have you been able to see past them?

My deepest desire growing up was to be counted among the beautiful. I truly believed if I was externally beautiful, I would finally be lovable. The problem was, my heart believed I was an ugly, unwanted dog. So no matter how beautiful I actually became, 'ugly' was all my eyes ever saw.

Remember, your eyes are filled with whatever is in your heart.

What do your eyes *want* to see more than anything when you look in the mirror? Do you desire beauty like I did? Do you desire health? Status and riches? Do you desire to see freedom, or someone worthy of being loved? Write your desires below.

_____

_____

Does it feel like those desires are unattainable or within your reach? Are you always unsatisfied with what you see?

_____

_____

_____

Could the lies and word daggers still inside of your heart be blurring your vision? If so, do you think it's possible for you to be filled with the truth so that you can see clearly?

_____

_____

_____

Our deep longing for beauty isn't a wrong desire. Every one of us is made in the image of a beautiful God, and our hearts simply yearn to look like Him! But the pain can poison the desire.

Think about your current state of beauty. Is it something you want, or something you could care less about? Is it defined by your reflection, or by the person that you are inside? Do you only feel beautiful if you can fit into your jeans, have clear skin, a good hair day, and appear to have it all together? Or does your heart feel beautiful, so beautiful is how you act? Take a few minutes and write out your thoughts on your beauty.

_____

_____

_____

How has the world's definition of beauty played into your perception of yourself? Do you compare yourself to people in magazines and on television, or maybe just the people around you? If you struggle with comparison, do you always feel unsatisfied?

_____

_____

_____

Think about your current state of self-respect. Do you feel like you need more notches on your belt before you're worthy of respect? Do you respect yourself?

_____

_____

_____

How has the world's words—through entertainment, media, movies, music, magazines, culture—influenced the tape measure you use to size yourself up? Do you believe you're good enough as you are? Could the world's definition about who you should be have a negative influence on your heart?

_____

_____

_____

_____

_____

_____

If your vision is blurry, I have a feeling there might be a few word daggers inside your heart that are influencing what you see. And until you remove those negative words and allow healing and truth, you're never going to see yourself as you truly are.

Take a minute to write out a prayer, asking God to start the heart-washing process, filling you with His words of truth that cast out all fear. Ask Him to help you see yourself through _His eyes_.

_____

_____

_____

_____

_____

_____

Day 2: Water World

Read 'Water' on pages 38-39.

Your body is made up of molecules, and liquid water is the most abundant molecule of all. In fact, the amount of water in a human ranges from 50-75%, making it the most substantial part of your physical makeup. Basically, you're a skin-colored water balloon, except you don't have to worry about bursting anytime soon.

After reading about Masaru Emoto's findings in _The Hidden Messages in Water_, take a moment and think about the water molecules inside the cells of your body. With every negative word spoken, those molecules change. And with every positive word spoken, those molecules respond. With every negative thought, the water molecules twist and contort, and with every thought of life, those molecules flow and flourish.

What do you think is going on with the water inside of your body? Is it calm, or is there a storm raging in there?

_____

_____

_____

Has your body of water had to endure a lot of negativity, from others and from yourself?

_____

_____

_____

_____

If so, have you had physical problems that might have come from your molecules enduring negative words and feelings over the years? Have you ever thought about your physical body responding to negativity before? _(Example: headaches, weight retention, ulcers, acne, etc.)_

_____

_____

_____

Take a moment below to draw out what you think your water molecules might look like inside your body at certain stages of your life.

Now, draw out what you *want* your molecules to look like.

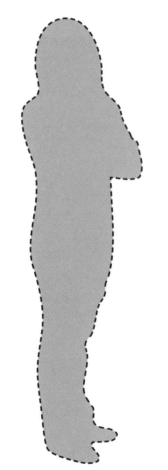

Your physical body can only survive three days without water. In order for you to stay alive, you have to actually pick up your cup and drink on a daily basis.

"If anyone thirsts,
let him come to me and drink.
Whoever believes in me, as the
Scripture has said,
'Out of his heart will flow rivers
of living water.'" John 7:37-38 (ESV)

In the same way you have to choose to drink water to keep your body alive, you have to choose to drink living water to keep your heart alive.

Take a minute to think about your heart being filled with living water. Jesus says that all you have to do is come and drink from His truth. Once you drink the cup of salvation— experiencing the living water of life—that truth is what naturally flows out of your life.

Do you need to take a drink of truth right now, and maybe keep drinking for a while? What does Jesus say about you that's been hard to believe? What scriptures or promises has He given that you need to put inside your cup and let your heart drink until you feel hydrated and alive?

Write truths that God has said about you in the cup. **Then take a minute, close your eyes, and imagine your heart taking a huge drink. Keep this list handy and begin to drink these truths every time your heart feels thirsty again.**

While Jesus was talking to the Samaritan woman in John 4:13-14, He made her a promise while talking to her at the well:

> *"Every one who drinks of this water will thirst again, but whoever drinks of the water that I shall give him will never thirst; the water that I shall give him will become in him a spring of water welling up to eternal life."* (NASB)

After reading this verse in college, I felt like a total failure as a Christian. I wondered why in the world my heart was still thirsty and struggling, especially since I'd taken a drink of Jesus. Why was this living water not working in my life? Why was salvation not a one-stop beverage where all my problems went away and living water flowed out of my life?

Have you ever felt like I did, wondering why living water isn't flowing out of your heart that might already be filled with Jesus?

_____

_____

The thing is, when you said yes to Christ and allowed Him to come and make a home inside your heart, a miracle happened. You went from having a thirsty heart to having everything you'd ever need—*with Jesus as your water source.*

You went from yearning for love to being filled with love!

If you're in Christ then the truth is, your heart is now a bubbling spring of living water. *Forever.*

But for many of us, it doesn't always *feel that way.*

Do you feel like your heart is a bubbling spring, overflowing with living water? Or do you feel like there are places that still need a good drink?

_____

_____

_____

If you're in Christ and you have Jesus in your heart, then draw your heart filled with this living water below.

And if you want to be filled with living water but you've never asked to take a drink, then ask Him now! Ask Him to come in, forgiving you, redeeming you, restoring you—so your heart will be reunited with the Love it was created for! If you're not ready, that's okay, too! **Draw the way your heart feels—does it feel full of living water, or cracked and dry?**

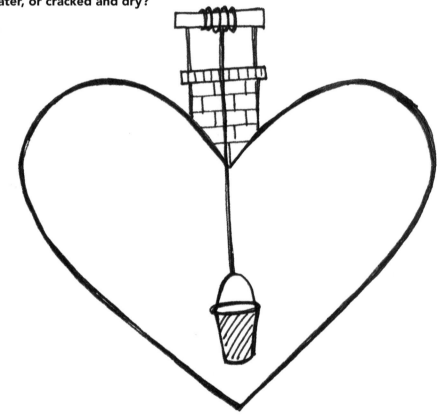

The thing about an underground spring is, the water isn't going to do you any good if you don't pick up a cup, draw up the water, and take a drink.

You see, for years I misinterpreted what Jesus was saying in John 4. He isn't saying that we never have to pick up our cups and drink again. He's saying that our cups will always be full because He is the source. He's saying that we don't ever have to thirst again, because...

we're now the water supply!

For years, my heart was full of living water, but I wasn't drinking the truth all day long! I wanted my moment of salvation to keep me hydrated for the course of my life, but that's not how water works.

For example, every day that I write, I bring a 1.5-liter of water with me and all day long, I take regular sips. Rarely, if ever, do I actually feel thirsty because I keep myself hydrated by drinking constantly. If your heart is full of living water, you're a bubbling spring, and Jesus lives inside of you. But you *still have to keep drinking from His well.*

Otherwise, your heart is going to get thirsty.

If you've stopped drinking from the bubbling spring Jesus has placed inside your heart, letting it water your life on a daily basis, write out a prayer below, asking Jesus to show you how to tip up your cup all day, every day.

_____

_____

_____

_____

_____

_____

_____

_____

_____

_____

_____

_____

Day 3: **Word Daggers**

Read 'Word Daggers' & 'What words have been spoken to you' on page 40.

Sticks and stones may break my bones, but man, words sure do kill. If I had the option to either let a kid hurl a rock at me, or hurl some of the words I've been called over the years, I'd take the rock any day.

Broken bones seem to heal a lot faster than a broken heart.

Take ten minutes and think about the words that have broken your heart, and in turn broken your life and list them below. These words were probably spoken by your family, your teachers, your friends, bullies, coaches, boyfriends and girlfriends. Unfortunately in this age of social media, online word daggers are everywhere, from critics to absolute strangers, hurling insults from the safety of their keyboards.

Words satisfy the mind as much as fruit does
the stomach; good talk is as gratifying as
a good harvest. Words kill, words give life;
they're either poison or fruit—you choose.
Proverbs 18: 20-21 (MSG)

Before you find yourself overwhelmed with how long your negative list might be, take a minute and thank yourself for facing some of the hardest word daggers that have slashed at your life. Nobody likes to look at painful memories where word daggers may have been thrust into our hearts, but in order to actually heal; these daggers must be removed and replaced with the truth.

Write a thank-you to yourself below, acknowledging the bravery, effort, and willingness to begin the surgery process of dagger removal.

_____

_____

_____

_____

_____

_____

_____

_____

_____

_____

Jesus, guard and protect each heart as they uncover the lies and let You go inside their hearts. I pray for healing, safety, and supernatural courage as they let the Doctor begin the surgery of dagger removal.

And Jesus, I pray that if some memories are too painful to resurface, that you would provide TRUTH in the days and weeks to come that would automatically kick out the lies!

Thank you, Father, that You're the best surgeon in the world, and You know exactly what You're doing. Thank you that it's not up to us to heal our own hearts—that You're way better at it than we ever could be. We open up our hearts to Your healing, to Your truth, and to Your life. Amen.

Day 4: **Word Power**

Read 'What words do you speak about yourself' on page 40.

Years ago as a newlywed, I was surprised one day when my Studhub very gently said to me, "Christa, do you realize how negative you talk to yourself when you're getting ready?"

I looked at him like he'd just told me the sky was pink.

Really? I thought. *Surely, he's wrong! I'm not a negative person!*

And then I started listening to myself. And what I found was shocking.

How normal is it in this day and age to put ourselves down in front of others, lightening the mood or even using ourselves as the brunt of a joke simply to get a laugh. We call ourselves things like stupid or idiot when we mess up or make a wrong turn, or use our mouths to agree with the things that we don't like about ourselves.

We stone our reflections in front of the mirror, treating ourselves worse than we'd treat an enemy!

If you believe that you're ugly, how is calling yourself 'ugly' every day going to ever change anything? If you've had an addictive personality in the past but don't like that about yourself, how is agreeing with that statement ever going to motivate freedom?

Let me clue you in on a little secret that someone told me...

a negative can only produce another negative.

Shaming yourself, criticizing, or judging your appearance and behavior *only keeps the ball rolling in the same direction.* If you ever truly want to change, you're going to have to change your speech.

Take several minutes and think about the words that you use to describe or talk to yourself. What are things you've said about yourself this week? What are the overarching themes? **Write every one of them below where you can see them.**

POSITIVE _____

NEGATIVE _____

_____   _____

_____   _____

_____   _____

_____   _____

Now, lets go at this from another angle. Ask someone who knows you best to be honest with you, cluing you in on the things they've heard you say about yourself. Ask your spouse, parents, coworkers and kids. (Kids are always brutally honest!). Find out if your perception is the same as theirs. You might be surprised just like I was.

POSITIVE _____   NEGATIVE _____

_____   _____

_____   _____

_____   _____

_____   _____

_____   _____

Where do you tend to say most of your negative words? Are they spewed out in front of people, or in front of your mirror?

_____

_____

_____

Sound is actual vibrations that pass through air, water, or other mediums. These vibrations might be invisible to your naked eye, but they always create substance.

What has the sound of your own voice created inside your heart? If you speak negatively about yourself on a regular basis, write down the substance that those words create. *(Example: insecurity, fear, self-hatred, depression, inadequacy, and illnesses)*

_____

_____

_____

A good man brings good things out of the good stored up in his heart, and an evil man brings evil things out of the evil stored up in his heart. For the mouth speaks what the heart is full of.
Luke 6:45 (NIV)

According to this scripture, it's not up to you to simply change your speech. You can't. Whatever is in your heart is going to come out of your mouth at some point, even if you try to muzzle yourself. Your responsibility is to take your heart to the Healer, letting His truth purify, cleanse, heal, and restore.

For years, I had a horrific anger problem. I'd memorize scriptures about patience and kindness, but the second my Studhub would do something remotely wrong; my eyes would see red and word daggers would spew out. Attempting to tame my tongue never worked, and neither did simply deciding to become a nice person.

I had to let the Healer begin to heal the hurt behind the anger—*and then my healed heart naturally spoke words of healing.*

If what's inside your heart is coming out of your mouth, then looking at your list of words, what's inside your heart? **Write your answers below.**

Now that you have a list of things you say about yourself and you've learned that those words are directly linked to the things in your heart, I want you to offer your heart to the Doctor again right now.

Father, trying to change my negative words won't work because they're linked to the pain in my heart. Trying to quit gossiping won't work. Trying to quit putting myself down won't work. Trying to quit snapping at my spouse and my kids won't work. I need the reasons behind the words to be uncovered and healed. I need a Doctor, a Healer, and a Savior. Come in again and have Your way. You have my permission to go into every corridor of my heart, redeeming, restoring, and breathing Your words of life. Do a deep work in me, God. The deepest work of all. I say yes to all You want to do. Amen.

Day 5: Word Healing

Read pages 41-42 in the 'Your Turn' section.

Today is a very important day. For today is the day you begin breaking old curses, replacing them with blessings.

Before you freak out at the word 'curse,' let's see what the Bible says about them for a moment.

> *Christ redeemed us from that self-defeating, cursed life by absorbing it completely into himself. Do you remember the Scripture that says, "Cursed is everyone who hangs on a tree"? That is what happened when Jesus was nailed to the cross: He became a curse, and at the same time dissolved the curse. And now, because of that, the air is cleared and we can see that Abraham's blessing is present and available for non-Jews, too. We are all able to receive God's life, his Spirit, in and with us by believing—just the way Abraham received it.*
> *Colossians 3:13-14* (MSG)

Translation—Good news people. The curse of sin and death has been broken by Jesus! He actually absorbed the whole thing into Himself at the cross, and now we get the fullness of the blessing of Abraham—receiving God's life, His Spirit—inside us and with us always and forever!

You are blessed and not cursed if you're in Christ!

Do you feel like your life has been blessed with this abundant life, or do you sometimes feel like you're still under a curse? Write your thoughts below.

_____

_____

_____

_____

For years, my life felt tormented by a curse that had already been broken. I felt cursed with self-hatred, addiction, insecurity, fear—and the list went on and on. I knew I was in Christ and a new creation in my *head*, but I sure didn't feel that way in my *heart*.

And then I learned how to *repent*.

Before you get a bad taste in your mouth from the word 'repentance,' let me explain scripturally what it really means.

The word *metanoia* comes from *meta*, meaning 'together with,' and *nous*, which means 'mind.' So basically, repentance is asking us to put our mind together with God's mind, believing what He says about us instead of what the world has said. This Greek word refers to a radical mind shift, realizing God's thoughts and words towards us!

This word "repentance" is actually a fabricated word that doesn't even exist in the original Greek text. It is taken from the Latin word, penance, with a 're' added to the front to emphasize a consciousness of sin. This error in translation led to the abusive doctrine of indulgences, where uneducated people were led to believe that they needed to purchase favor from an angry God.

Francouis du Toit writes in his translation of scripture called *The Mirror Bible*:

"English translations do little to help us understand what repentance truly is. Until Jerome's Latin Vulgate translation, the word 'metanoia' was commonly used. For instance, Tertullian wrote in 198 A.D., "In Greek, 'metanoia' is not a confession of sins, but a change of mind." But despite this, the Latin fathers begin to translate the words as "do penance" following the Roman Catholic teaching on doing penance in order to win God's favor."

Have you had a version of 'repentance' more in line with the original Greek 'metanoia' —to radically shift your mind to be like God's mind—or more like the mistranslated version where we pay penance in order to win God's favor?

_____

_____

Take a moment to meditate on this new definition of 'repentance.' Do you think it's possible to truly repent and align your mind and heart with what God thinks and says about you?

_____

_____

_____

You've made two lists this week.
> 1) The list of word daggers that people have said about you.
> 2) The list of word daggers you've said about yourself.

It's time to repent for those lists, allowing dagger removal in your heart as you come into agreement with the truth.

For each negative, slashing word that's been spoken and wounded your heart, take a moment and ask the Holy Spirit to speak to your spirit, finding out what He says. Let the Doctor's medicine of truth begin to fill the corridors of pain—bringing life, truth, and healing. You can't simply tell yourself you're beautiful and expect your broken heart to believe it. **You need to hear *Him* say it.**

And if you're afraid you can't hear, then quickly 'repent' and come into agreement with what God says about you in John 10:27:

> *"My sheep hear my voice, and I know*
> *them, and they follow me"* (NKJV)

If you're a sheep, then you hear your master. If you don't think you're a sheep, ask to be one. If you want to hear and don't think you can, then open the scriptures. They're right there in front of you full of the truth.

The words that have ruined your life need to be replaced with words that are going to restore your life. And you need to see them and say them until the medicine of those words kicks out the lies.

Take as long as you need to hear the truth, writing out each word below.

WORD DAGGERS

HEALING WORDS

_____   _____

_____   _____

_____   _____

_____   _____

_____   _____

_____   _____

_____   _____

_____   _____

WORD DAGGERS

HEALING WORDS

_____   _____

_____   _____

_____   _____

_____   _____

_____   _____

_____   _____

_____   _____

_____   _____

_____   _____

_____   _____

_____   _____

Now that you have your repentance list—the list that's going to radically shift your mind and heart—it's time to go to war. You might have had years, possibly decades, letting negative words wound and define your life. Which is why for the next forty days, you're going to declare God's truth—letting His words define your life. You've heard Him tell you the truth, and now you're going to come into agreement with it.

So, beautiful friend, open up your mouth and let the medicine go deep. It's time to heal.

Week 3: **GROUP DISCUSSION QUESTIONS**

Chapter 2: Sticks and Stones

1 **Begin with a prayer, thanking God for the lies that He's uncovering and the truth that He's restoring.** Declare John 8:32, that *"the truth will set you free."*

2 **Read the 'We Believe God Can' list aloud.** Set your expectation on what God promises He's done, not what your week might have looked like. Briefly give any testimony of your declarations blooming to life over the past week.

3 **Discussion Questions:**

• When God created the world, He spoke, and life came into existence. Words create either life or death, which means, there's no gray speech. Take a minute and discuss the weightiness of words and how they create.

• What are some of the negative words said to you over the years that you've partnered with and made a part of your belief system? How have those words altered your life?

• How did it feel to realize that you'd given your power to unqualified sources?

• What are things you've become accustomed to speaking over yourself that you shouldn't, even if they appear to be true?

• Your body is made up of seventy percent water, and as you learned, the molecules in water respond to words in a negative or positive way. What has your physical body had to endure over the years under the weight of negative words?

• As a group, repent (which means to 'rethink'), and ask God to let you hear what He says about you. Commit to hearing the truth and then declaring it aloud over your own life.

• Share one thing from your declaration list that you're committing to speak over your life for the next forty days.

4 **Close with a prayer, declaring that God will fulfill His promise of freedom for every heart.**

5 **Have *Chapter 3* and the assignments completed by the next time you meet. (Pages 44-67)**

week four
Chapter 3 Puddle Jumping

Day 1: **Connect the Dots**

Read pages 47-65 in *God Loves Ugly*.

As I looked in the mirror today, a thought crossed my mind: *I could play connect the dots with the blemish situation happening on my forehead and chin.* After my daughter Goldie died in my arms just three short months ago, I decided since it was the first time in years that I wasn't either pregnant or nursing, I should probably do some sort of a cleanse.

Well, let's just say the cleanse is working, as evidenced by my skin. Those nasty toxins releasing in my body have to go somewhere, and of all the places to go, they picked my face.

Awesome.

I quickly put on concealer that did little to hide the red mountain range underneath, threw on some lipstick, and headed out the door. Hours later when I ran to the bathroom, I looked up at my face while washing my hands.

Hmmmm, I thought. *I totally forgot about my connect the dot situation—proving that people really can change and miracles do happen!*

When things in the mirror aren't exactly what you want, do you forget about the imperfections when you walk away from the mirror, or do you carry emotional baggage into your day?

_____

_____

Years ago, the connect the dots situation on my face would have ruined my day—hijacking my emotions and taking them hostage. I would have felt insecure, ugly, and ashamed. I would have felt embarrassed and acutely aware of my lack of perfection, tortured by each moment. But I can honestly say without a shadow of a doubt, I finally connected the right dots and put the right information together: my emotions are choices.

I have the power to choose whether or not I act on them.

Would you consider yourself a very emotional person like me, or do your emotions have a hard time coming to the surface? Rate yourself on the chart below.

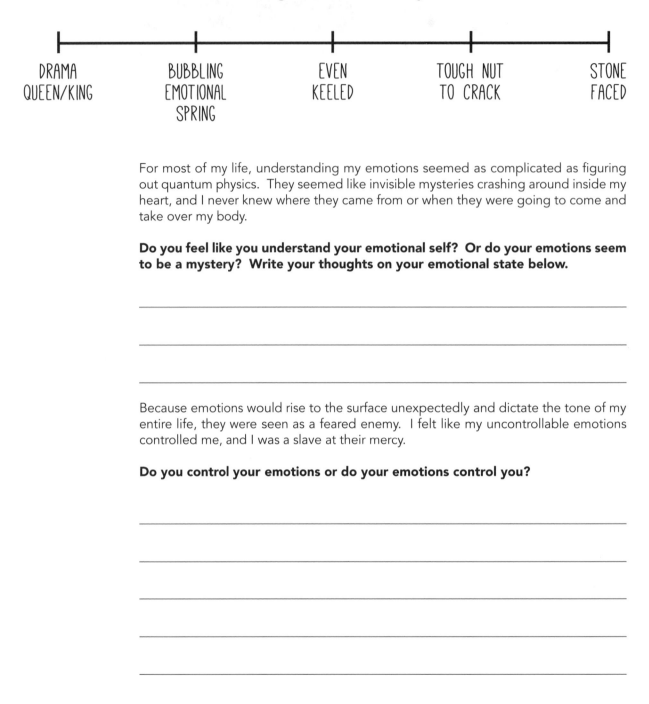

DRAMA QUEEN/KING	BUBBLING EMOTIONAL SPRING	EVEN KEELED	TOUGH NUT TO CRACK	STONE FACED

For most of my life, understanding my emotions seemed as complicated as figuring out quantum physics. They seemed like invisible mysteries crashing around inside my heart, and I never knew where they came from or when they were going to come and take over my body.

Do you feel like you understand your emotional self? Or do your emotions seem to be a mystery? Write your thoughts on your emotional state below.

_____

_____

_____

Because emotions would rise to the surface unexpectedly and dictate the tone of my entire life, they were seen as a feared enemy. I felt like my uncontrollable emotions controlled me, and I was a slave at their mercy.

Do you control your emotions or do your emotions control you?

_____

_____

_____

_____

_____

_____

I always think it's funny when people are scared of emotions being involved when experiencing God. If you believe you're created in His image then guess what—God is extremely emotional, as evidenced throughout the Bible! In fact, two out of the three descriptions He wants you to enjoy in this new kingdom available in Christ are emotional states.

> *"For the kingdom of God is not a matter of eating and drinking but of righteousness and peace and joy in the Holy Spirit." Romans 14:17* (ESV)

When my Studhub Lucas and I were falling in love, there were moments when he'd look at me and I thought my physical body would explode into a million pieces. The emotion of love was so powerful; it would send my entire body to a cosmic state of pure bliss.

So if God doesn't just love—if He *is* love—then don't you think He might have created your emotions to help you experience Him? Beautiful friend, our emotions are from God, and God gives us access to love, joy, peace, patience, kindness, goodness, faithfulness, gentleness, self-control—even anger, rage, grief, and sorrow just to name a few. If these gifts called emotions are from Him and He has emotions Himself, could they actually help our lives, instead of hurt them? Could God have created good emotions to build us up instead of tear us down?

Take a few minutes and write out your thoughts about emotions being from God. Do you need to start looking at them from another angle if they might have been seen as an enemy?

_____

_____

_____

_____

_____

_____

_____

Father, thank you for my emotions. I bring them to You now—the good and the bad. There's nothing going on inside my heart that You can't handle. There's no storm too great that You can't calm and bring peace. I believe You can teach me to be a healthy emotional being, as evidenced in Your word.

I submit my emotions to You now. Have Your way, Your peace, joy, and love inside of my heart. Amen.

Day 2: **Perfect Peace**

Read 'What Emotions Do You Primarily Feel' on pages 66-67.

Whether you ranked yourself as a drama queen or stone faced in the last lesson, all of us have an emotional identity. Drama queens might have an easier time pinpointing what's going on in there because it spews out all the time, but even stone faces have a lot happening under the surface that can't be seen. Our hearts were never meant to be void of emotion—even if they've grown cold over time in protection from pain.

How many little boys are told to man up and quit crying because of some silly notion that men shouldn't feel? How many little girls are told to chill out because they're 'too much' while learning how to express themselves on an emotional rant?

What have you been told over the years that might have negatively affected your emotional identity?

_____

_____

_____

How would you describe your emotional identity? Do you feel like you're full of healthy emotions, or are plagued by ones that make your soul sick?

_____

_____

_____

Emotions aren't our enemies—in fact, the right ones are full of medicine that heal us. Love, joy, and peace continue to release healing from my heart into every part of my life.

> *"But the fruit of the Spirit is love, joy,*
> *peace, patience, kindness, goodness,*
> *faithfulness, gentleness, self-control..."*
> *Galatians 5:22-23 9* (NASB)

If you're in Christ then I have news for you—*these tasty fruits already live inside of you.* You don't have to find peace; you already have it growing freely inside your heart. You don't have to find joy; you already have access to an abundant supply. You don't have to be filled with love—Love has made His home inside your heart, and He's never leaving based upon your behavior! Instead of the fruit of the Spirit and the love of God being something to attain, they're gifts inside your heart because of *who* lives inside your heart.

And it might be time to pick up these fruits and let your heart take a bite.

Take a few minutes and be quiet. Make sure you're not distracted by music, television, kids or responsibilities. Close your eyes and take a deep breath. As you inhale, imagine a big golden cup filled with liquid peace. Pick up that cup, and let your heart take a big, fat drink of the peace that passes understanding, asking it to guard your heart and mind in Christ. (Philippians 4:7)

Now that you see how full your heart is, imagine a bubbling spring of peace deep inside. As you inhale, the spring bubbles up. As you exhale, it begins to overflow into your mind, your body, and your emotions. Stay in this spring of peace for at least five minutes, but I guarantee you—you'll want to stay forever. Set your alarm if you need to, but stay in the spring the entire time.

After five minutes have passed, write your experience, feelings, and thoughts.

_____

_____

_____

_____

_____

_____

_____

Is this feeling of peace one that you'd like to experience on a regular basis, maybe staying there forever? Do you think that remaining in peace, even as the storms of life rage, is possible?

_____

_____

_____

_____

Does living in a perpetual state of peace seem as impossible as trying to hike to the moon? Write your thoughts below.

_____

_____

_____

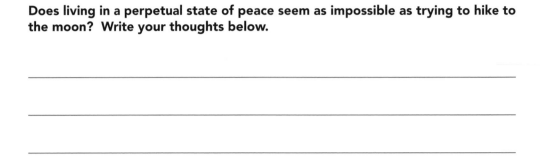

*"On that day, when evening had come, he said to them, 'Let us go across to the other side.' And leaving the crowd, they took him with them in the boat, just as he was. And other boats were with him. And a great storm of wind arose, and the waves beat into the boat, so that the boat was already filling. **But he was in the stern, asleep on the cushion;** and they woke him and said to him, 'Teacher, do you not care if we perish?' And he awoke and rebuked the wind, and said to the sea, 'Peace! Be still!' And the wind ceased, and there was a great calm. He said to them, 'Why are you afraid? Have you no faith?' And they were filled with awe, and said to one another, 'Who then is this, that even wind and sea obey him?'" Mark 4:35-41*

Jesus didn't come to earth to show us how awesome He is and how lacking we are. He came to show us all that's available to us *because of Him*. If Jesus is a storm sleeper, then guess what—you can be a storm sleeper, too. He had so much faith in His Father—in the promises of God—those promises were like weighted concrete anchoring His heart to peace. And that peace on the inside of Him was so great, He could fall asleep when all hell was breaking loose! His inner atmosphere defined His outer world, so much so, that He could stand up and speak to a physical storm, and that storm would stop!

Your inner atmosphere affects your outer world.

Last week as I began the grueling task of packing up our belongings to move houses for what seemed like the millionth time in several years, my heart felt completely overwhelmed. As the nasty feeling arose inside, the whole house shifted and I could feel an actual buzz of anxiety, electric in the air. As I huffed around in frustration at the task ahead of me, my little two-year-old son Moses started running around hitting things with a baseball bat, screaming his little head off.

Realizing what was happening, I took a deep breath, reconnected with my inheritance of peace already inside my heart, and offered a silent prayer from Isaiah 26:3 *"You will keep in perfect peace all who trust in you, all whose thoughts are fixed on you!"* (NLT) Bending down to pick up my son, I sang into his ear, prayed over his little heart, and released the peace inside of me over his life.

And within seconds, my inner peace defined his entire world.

If the emotional atmosphere in your heart releases something in your world, do you feel like you calm storms, or create them?

_____

_____

_____

In the picture below, draw the primary emotions you can pinpoint that reside inside of your heart. Write the main ones in big letters in the center, and the secondary emotions closer to the outside.

Go back to the picture above. If your inner atmosphere defines your outer world, then **draw a line from each emotion to what that emotion creates outside your heart.** Does your inner peace release relationship and connection? Does your worry release anxiety, nail biting, and micromanaging? Does your insecurity release fear, perfectionism, or shyness? Does your joy release laughter and life? **Take a few moments and draw what's created because of the emotions inside your heart.**

Jesus, seal each heart today with Your promises. Fill each heart with peace, love, joy, hope, and life. And as the ugly parts of our hearts are exposed, You're right there to remove, replace, and restore. We believe that You will do all You say You will do. Amen.

Day 3: **The Tree of Life**

Read 'What Experiences Are Behind The Emotions' on pages 66-67.

Imagine, if you will, a large oak tree.

This tree didn't start out stretching to the sky—it began as a tiny seed planted in fertile soil. As the seed was fueled with water and sunlight, a root system grew until a tiny trunk began to surface above the ground. With the right weather conditions year after year, the trunk of the tree continued to grow strong and steady, adding large branches and leaves.

After many seasons of withstanding all sorts of storms, this oak tree has become so strong; it's not going anywhere.

Let's break down the components of this large oak tree for just a moment using my childhood story of being called an ugly dog in Chapter 2.

SEED: The painful **experience** of rejection planted a seed inside the fertile soil of my heart.

ROOTS: And as I watered the seed of rejection with my **thoughts**, a root system began to grow.

TRUNK: The thoughts of rejection helped to solidify **beliefs**, and a trunk began to appear from the ground.

BRANCHES: The more I allowed rejected thoughts and beliefs to grow inside my heart, the branches of **emotions** grew everywhere.

Before I knew it, my unhealed, painful experience with those boys that day in middle school led to unworthy thoughts that solidified as beliefs, and I found myself a hot mess of uncontrollable emotions.

EMOTIONS

BELIEFS

THOUGHTS

EXPERIENCE

Go back to page 67 where you pinpointed the emotions inside your heart, focusing on the negatives that have set up residence inside. On the tree below, work backwards from each negative emotion, asking God to help you pinpoint the beliefs, thoughts, and experiences where those emotions began.

BRANCHES / EMOTIONS

_____
_____
_____
_____

TRUNKS / BELIEFS

_____
_____
_____
_____

ROOTS / THOUGHTS

_____
_____
_____

SEEDS / EXPERIENCES

_____
_____
_____
_____

Now that you can actually see the origin of your negative emotions, they don't seem as overwhelming, do they? Once you realize that they have a *source*, it's easier to see how if the source is healed, the emotions can change.

Go back to your emotional heart on page 67, writing out the positive feelings you experience. On the tree below, work backwards from each emotion, asking God to help you pinpoint the beliefs, thoughts, and experiences where they all began.

BRANCHES / EMOTIONS

_____

_____

_____

_____

TRUNKS / BELIEFS

_____

_____

_____

_____

ROOTS / THOUGHTS

_____

_____

_____

_____

SEEDS / EXPERIENCES

_____

_____

Dear friend, there's always an experience behind each emotion. You didn't just wake up angry one day. You didn't just come out of the womb insecure. You didn't just zap into fear. And on the positive side, there's a lifetime that led you to be rooted in love, joy, peace, and trust.

If **negative experiences** led to **negative beliefs** producing **negative emotions**, then your heart needs to heal from the pain of the initial experience, otherwise, nothing ever changes. And I know a great Healer who can do just that. This Healer loves to manifest actual, **positive experiences** with His love, leading to **positive beliefs**, naturally producing **positive emotions.**

Your responsibility isn't to change your negative emotions—you can't. They come from pain inside your heart. Your responsibility is to take the pain to a Healer, and out of the experience you have with Him, life begins to grow.

If you've tried and tried to change your emotional identity with little or no results, take a moment right now and surrender again. Stop trying to stabilize your feelings—submit your heart to the Doctor.

God, I surrender my emotional heart to You, right now. You created this emotional self inside of me, and it's not the enemy. Negative emotions are not the enemy—they simply come from pain. I submit the pain in my heart, once again, to you, Healer. I need an experience with Your love that's greater than my experiences with pain. I need an experience with Your acceptance that's greater than my rejection. Meet me now. Hold me close. Love me into wholeness. Amen.

Day 4: Perfect Love

Read 'What Are You Afraid Of' on page 67.

When your first memories of life were sexual like mine were, you're bound to have some cracks in the foundation of your heart. But all the little cracks that surfaced over the years weren't the real problem—they were the result of an enormous root growing deep inside.

The root of *fear.*

For the majority of my life, my heart was fueled by fear—fear of rejection, fear of intimacy, fear of failure. I struggled with fear of success, fear of being seen and known, fear of being found out. Fear was a terrible motivator, a slave driving me towards perfectionism. Fear was paralyzing, crippling me from becoming who I wanted to be.

You don't need to have been abused like I was for fear to have sneaked its way inside. Fear grows like a weed behind neglect, rejection, and abandonment—even circumstantial situations like poverty, culture and religion, divorce, overbearing parents, or being bullied.

1. Is fear motivating you towards achievement and success? Are you afraid you're not going to measure up to your parent's standards, society's standards, or your own?

2. Has fear been paralyzing, keeping you locked away from love, dreaming, or even trying? Has fear caused depression, addiction, or reclusive behaviors?

Write your answers in the boxes below.

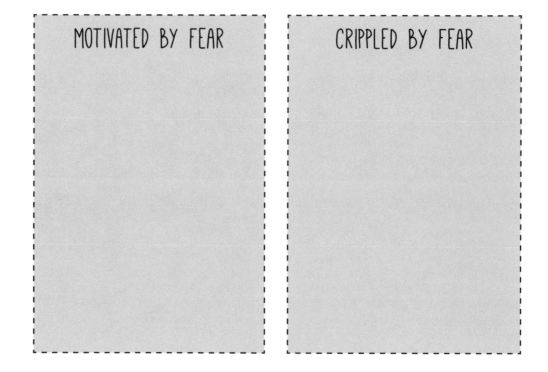

MOTIVATED BY FEAR

CRIPPLED BY FEAR

Your deepest desire as a human being is to be loved and accepted. Remember, you're created in the image of *Love*. When you've had experiences that left you lacking love, longing for love, or abused by perverted love, I guarantee you, fear got its foot in the door of your heart.

There is no fear in love, but perfect love casts out fear. I John 4:18

For years, I tried to get rid of my fear. I'd tried to kick it out of my heart, starve it, and will it away. But the crazy thing about fear is, it can't be pulled out. It has to be displaced.

If you struggle with fear in any capacity, write 'FEAR' to the right inside the love bucket of your heart.

Remember in I John 4:18 where it says *perfect love casts out fear?* According to this scripture, draw a picture in the love bucket to the right of how you might cast out fear.

Friend, you can't get rid of your fear. You can only pour love over it until love casts it out.

Your responsibility isn't to deal with your fear. Your responsibility is to let yourself be loved.

The next time I get pregnant, I guarantee fear is going to come knocking at my heart. When you've carried a baby to term and that baby died in your arms, trauma is a breeding ground for fear if it's not dealt with properly. In the last three months since my little Luca Gold left this earth, fear has tried, on many occasions, to get a root inside my heart.

But when the very natural thoughts of fear have come, plaguing me with questions of how it might happen again, I've had a strategy that actually works.

I stop. I take a deep breath. I physically lift my eyes to the heavens and scream out inside my heart...

"Love me, Jesus. Love me until this fear is kicked out and Your love is all that remains."

Before I know what's happened, I'm filled with love, the presence of God, my eyes are fixed on Jesus, and fear gets displaced by the God of the universe who lives in me. I submit myself to love, and love deals with my fear. I submit myself to God, and God deals with my fear.

If you struggle with fear, take at least five minutes and submit yourself to love. If you need to, look up at the sky and lift your eyes to Jesus. If you need to lie down and imagine a big bucket of love pouring into your heart, then imagine it like a waterfall until it feels real. Let yourself be loved right now—let love be your healer. Let love be your liberator. Let love be your freedom.

Write your experience below.

_____

_____

_____

_____

_____

_____

_____

_____

_____

_____

_____

Father, thank you for Your love that comes to set the captives free! We receive ALL You have for us today, whether we feel worthy of it or not! We say 'yes and amen' to Your unconditional love that kicks out our fear! Amen.

Day 5: **The Physical Link**

Read 'The Physical Link' pages 63-64.

When I wrote *God Loves Ugly* in 2010, I knew there was a physical link between our emotions and our physical being, but I didn't have the scientific evidence. I just knew in my own life, my self-hatred kept manifesting in the form of acne, rashes, blotchy skin and headaches. Even as a small child when the pain from my abuse and inadequacy would overwhelm my heart, my body would physically shut down and I would pass out. For a while, it seemed as if I was battling seizures, but after a while, doctors began pulling my mother aside at the hospital and telling her to get me checked out by a psychologist.

The pain in my heart was so intense; it was physically shutting down my body.

Imagine what the emotions of self-hatred have done to your physical body over the years. Imagine what fear has released into your cells. As we learned in Week 1, Dr. Caroline Leaf lets us know in her book *Who Switched Off My Brain*, fear alone triggers more than 1400 chemical and physical responses and activates more than thirty hormones.

We all know we can be hormonal, ladies. But instead of being at the mercy of our hormones, what if some of those hormones are actually released *because of our emotions*, and not the other way around?

Are you currently struggling with physical issues of any kind? Have you had physical issues in the past? If so, write them below.

_____

_____

_____

After every stressful semester in college, I would come home and immediately get sick. And every year after getting off of a difficult or taxing musical tour, I'd get home and my body would fall ill. It was almost as if all the stress, lack of sleep, and anxiety from the tough situations would release the moment I rested, and my body would physically crash as a result.

Take a minute and see if you can notice patterns between illness and stress. Have you ever thought much about emotions and thoughts being behind certain sicknesses, diseases, or toxins in your body? Write any patterns or connections you see below.

_____

_____

_____

"Trust in the Lord with all your heart,
and do not rely on your own insight.
In all your ways acknowledge him,
and he will make straight your paths.
Be not wise in your own eyes;
fear the Lord, and turn away from evil.
*It will be **healing to your flesh***
*and **refreshment to your bones.***"*
Proverbs 3:5-8

Scripture promises us that trusting God with all our hearts, acknowledging Him, revering Him and turning from evil will *manifest physically in our bodies.* Trust heals our actual flesh and refreshes our bones.

"My son, be attentive to my words;
incline your ear to my sayings.
Let them not escape from your sight;
keep them within your heart.
For they are life to him who finds them,
and healing to all his flesh."
Proverbs 4:20-22

The truth of God's words, when kept inside our hearts, brings life and healing *to our physical bodies.*

"Pleasant words are like a honeycomb,
sweetness to the soul and health to the body."
Proverbs 16:24

Pleasant words in the soul actually bring *health to the body.*

The same way that lies, fear, and negativity fuel sickness and death, God's truth and words inside our hearts brings healing and life to our physical bodies. His desire and intention for us on this earth is to walk in healing and wholeness, in every sense of the word, including our physical bodies.

And it starts with our thought life, and the beliefs in our hearts.

If your emotions have wreaked havoc on your physical body over the years, it's time to bring those emotions to the Healer and ask Him to heal your body as He heals your heart.

Take a few minutes and bring your body to the Healer, asking Him to give you a strategy for health and wholeness in your body. And if you already have health, then ask Him for a strategy to maintain all you've been blessed with.

Write out what He tells you below.

_____

_____

_____

_____

_____

_____

_____

_____

_____

_____

_____

Father, You want our bodies healed along with our minds and hearts. I bring my body before You today asking You to fuse Your truth deep inside, bringing healing and health to my body. I ask You to reset me chemically, that Your truth would resound down to the cellular level of my DNA. I ask that You would speed up the process in my mind, reconnecting pathways that naturally fire truth in my brain. I want my whole spirit, soul, and body to be in sync with Your truth, Your healing, and Your life. Amen.

week
four
Discussion

Week 4: GROUP DISCUSSION QUESTIONS

Chapter 3: Puddle Jumping

1 **Begin with a prayer, agreeing with Jeremiah 29:11. That God has a future and a hope for each of you.**

2 **Read the 'We Believe God Can' list aloud.** Set your expectation on what God promises He's done, not what you haven't been able to do. Briefly give any testimony of your declarations blooming to life over the past week.

3 **Discussion Questions:**
• Has everyone declared the truth this week? Hold one another accountable for the duration of the study. Give a testimony!

• Talk about the origin of emotions—how experiences form beliefs, and beliefs create feelings. Are you extremely emotional and never knew why? Have you ever thought about where your emotions came from?

• What is the most common emotion that you experience? (joy, peace, fear, anxiety, insecurity, frustration, contentment). Why do you believe you experience that more than anything else?

• Fear is one of the most common negative emotions. What has fear done for your life? What does scripture say is the only way to get rid of fear?

• I John 4:18 says that "Perfect love casts out all fear." Do you believe this is possible? What are some practical ways to do this?

• Emotions can affect our physical bodies. Has your body manifested your negative emotions? (Insomnia, acne, ulcers, etc.)

• Talk about why you believe God created emotions. What would it look like to live in your inheritance of joy, peace, and hope on a daily basis?

4 **Close with a prayer, declaring that God will fulfill His promise of freedom for every heart.**

5 **Have *Chapter 4* and the assignments completed by the next time you meet. (Pages 68-85)**

week five
Chapter 4 There's Always a Reason

Day 1: **God & Sex**

Read 'There's Always A Reason' on pages 71-73.

You are a sexual being. And because you're created in the image of God, you don't have anything inside your makeup that doesn't come from Him. *Which means, God created sexuality, sex, pleasure, and all that comes with it.*

In Genesis when God created the earth, the Trinity was already in existence, having full relationship, intimacy, and fellowship inside the three-in-one. And within the love and relationship they had among themselves, the Trinity decided to birth life.

Intimacy gave birth to life, and mankind was formed. God had kids out of love—and you're one of them.

God's intention and will for mankind is that relationship and intimacy with Him would give birth to all sorts of life on this earth—life in relationships, life in abundance, life in creation. Marriage was His idea and is a reflection of that unity that produces life, where man and woman come together in intimacy, with pleasure, that gives birth to creation.

Sex is from God. It was His idea and He created it. Which means no matter what you've been taught, it's not *bad or shameful.*

The enemy has done a great job claiming sex as his creation and making it a 'worldly thing.' If he can pervert the sexual in someone's life, and pleasure becomes self-gratifying instead of intimately life giving, then sin and death are produced. If he can keep us from believing that sex is from God, that it's dirty or wrong, then we stay shameful while doing it—even inside marriage.

I know this first hand.

As a small child when the sexual was turned on far too early from abuse outside the home, sex was a horrible thing. My feelings of sexuality were shameful. They were dirty. They were to be hidden. They made me gross. They led to years of self-gratification as a bondage and addiction, and intimacy became perverted and wrong.

Take a moment and write out your thoughts about sex, sexuality, and intimacy. Has sex been perverted because of the past? Has sex been something you've never enjoyed, or maybe never had? Has sex been something dirty and wrong? Has sex been a life-giving part of your covenant relationship? Is it something you have to do out of duty or out of love?

_____

_____

_____

How has the world's view on sex influenced your beliefs? Has the church or Christianity had any education or been of any help to your sexual identity? Where did you get your sexual perspective?

_____

_____

_____

_____

Did your parents talk about sex in the home, or was it something that you had to figure out on your own? Did it seem shameful and secret, or something that was good and intimate?

_____

_____

_____

If statistics are correct, sexual abuse is a monster devouring our children. There are estimated to be 42 million adult survivors of sexual abuse in the U.S. alone, with 1 in 4 women and 1 in 6 men sexually abused before the age of eighteen.[1] Abused children are 25% more likely to become pregnant as a teen, and as many as two-thirds of the people in treatment for drug abuse reported being abused or neglected as a child.[2]

Needless to say, there's always more than meets the eye when someone is showing destructive external behaviors. That's why simply treating the behavior never works.

The heart must be healed before the behavior can permanently change.

There are many ways that the sexual realm can affect us. You might not have been abused like I was, but maybe you slept around a lot in your early years or did things you regretted. Maybe you've struggled with pornography or a perverted and lustful thought life. Maybe you've stayed far from the sexual world and feel completely shut down in that area. Or maybe you're just fine, healthy as can be in the area of sex.

Sources:
(1) http://cachouston.org/child-sexual-abuse-facts/
(2) http://www.childhelp.org/pages/statistics

On the chart below, take a moment and rate where you are as a sexual being. Does sex feel like it brings life within intimacy? Or has sex poisoned your life like a plague?

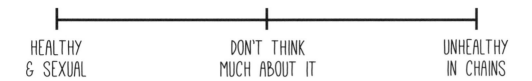

The reason I'm talking about the sexual world at the beginning of this chapter is because I believe it's one of the most important factors in your life. Sex was created by God to create intimacy and life—and you're a sexual being whether or not you're having sex. If you've dealt with sexual shame—abuse, promiscuity, perversion, addiction, pornography, lust, cheating—then I guarantee you, life will cease in places of your heart until the root of the pain is healed.

Do you carry sexual shame? Maybe shame from religion, or from abuse, masturbation, promiscuity, lust, pornography, cheating, or maybe an abortion? Do you carry sexual fear—afraid of it or ashamed you've never had it? If so, take a moment and write the shame and fear that you carry below.

_____

_____

_____

Romans 8:1 says "There is therefore now no condemnation for those who are in Christ Jesus." So if God doesn't have any condemnation for you, then why would you have any for yourself or for others?

Take a moment and write out a prayer, surrendering any shame, guilt, or condemnation you might be carrying about sex. Get it all off your chest and out of your heart. This isn't a load you can continue to haul around while trying to heal.

_____

_____

_____

Unhealed wounds from my abuse led to all sorts of addictions and depression in the early years, eventually bringing that same dysfunction into my marriage. Intimacy was perverted, so when it finally became pure, my body would physically shut down because it didn't know what to do. It took years to try and untangle the mess inside my heart where my body would work properly inside the covenant of marriage.

If our sexual identity isn't addressed as we try to get our hearts healed, then a huge part of the foundation of our lives goes unnoticed.

And that's just not good enough. Especially when Jesus came that we might be whole—in our spirit, soul, and body.

Take a moment and get quiet before God. Ask Him to scan your heart, doing a sexual health scan.   Start talking to Him about your sexual wellbeing. There is more work to be done, but get the cards on the table and open up the subject for discussion.

God created intimacy, and intimacy gives birth to life. Life is His intention for you—in every area, including the sexual realm.

If talking to a God you can't see is hard, then do what I do. Pour two cups of coffee and sit across from an empty chair and start talking. You might get kicked out of a coffee shop if you do it in public, so either talk in your head, or hold up your phone and have a conversation with Someone on the other end. God doesn't need a cell phone, but I promise He's listening and loves to answer our questions. If that seems weird, then take the space below and begin to journal, writing Him a letter about the sexual realm. Talk about how you feel, what's happened to you, and things you think can never change.

Make sure you don't do all the talking. Give space to listen, leaning your heart in to hear what He has to say. I guarantee you; He has *no* condemnation for you, no matter what you've done. Write down your experience below.

_____

_____

_____

_____

_____

_____

Jesus, thank you that You heal everything—even a sexual past that has perverted true intimacy. You heal everything—even the longings for intimacy that haven't been fulfilled yet. We submit ourselves to You as sexual beings that You created. You have an intention and a will for us to work the way that You created us—to have oneness and intimacy that gives birth to life!

We submit our hearts, souls, and bodies to You now. HAVE YOUR WAY. Do Your work. Make us clean and whole as sexual beings. Amen.

Day 2: **Spirit, Soul, Body**

Read 'Body, Soul, Spirit' on pages 74-76.

Over the course of my life, I'd always heard about people being made up of a body, soul, and spirit, living in that order. But if you're in Christ, you get to live a little differently.

"Now may the God of peace Himself sanctify you entirely; and may your spirit and soul and body be preserved complete, without blame at the coming of our Lord Jesus Christ."
I Thessalonians 5:23 (NAS)

As a Christian, your inheritance is for God to preserve you in peace, and it involves living spirit, soul, to body, in that order.

Do you feel like you live primarily in your body, or your soul? Or do you abide in your spirit, connected with God?

In the outline to the right, write the three words 'spirit, soul, and body' in their order of priority in your life.

If you feed your body too much, it will gain weight. If you feed your soul too much, it will puff up. And if you feed your spirit too much, you become the best version of yourself, preserved in peace and connected with the God of the universe, being led into all truth. (John 16:13)

After reading about the components of each part in *God Loves Ugly*, how much do you feed each part? Which one is the biggest and which one is the smallest? Choose which picture below represents your body, which one is your soul, and which one is your spirit. Write the words on each picture and the amount of time you devote to each of them.

If your body is a house carrying around the most precious cargo—you—then how much importance do you put on it? Do you spend the majority of your time worrying about it, grooming it, or making it perfect? Do you neglect it? Are you ashamed of it? Is it your enemy? Do you keep it healthy and whole through diet and exercise within moderation? Write out your thoughts about your body below.

_____

_____

_____

_____

_____

_____

Your soul is the mainframe computer of who you are. It's where you think; it's where you feel, and where you make your decisions. It contains your personality and your character. And it remembers *everything*. It holds onto all the pain, trauma, abuse, neglect, and every negative—even if you've suppressed it within your memories.

Is your soul in pretty good shape, or is it still beat up from the past? Does it feel healthy, or still wounded? Do you give much thought to your soul, or does your soul feel like it constantly destroys you? Ask God to give you a soul scan for a moment and write your thoughts below.

_____

_____

_____

_____

_____

Your spirit is the part of you that connects with the God of the universe. It's where you hear His voice, where He communes with you, where He heals your heart.

Do you feel like your spirit is empty, or filled? Do you feel like it's hard to connect with God, or extremely easy? Write your answers about your spirit below.

The reality is, if you said yes to Jesus you became a new creation. Your old, sinful nature was *crucified and no longer lives, but Christ lives in you.* (Galatians 2:20) It's dead. You've been resurrected with Christ and seated in heavenly places. (Ephesians 2:6) But when you got saved, God didn't wipe out your memory of all the things that happened to wound your soul over the years.

Your soul remembers everything, *doesn't it?*

The reason I found it so hard to live in the spirit for many, many years was because my soul was always screaming. Loudly. The pain in my heart needed constant attention, always hungry for something to numb it, medicate it, or stuff it down even further. And I had no idea how to **submit the pain in my soul to the Healer already in my spirit.**

But there is a way.

And if it worked for me, it will work for you, too—not because of us, but because of who lives in us.

Take a few moments and submit your body to your soul, and your soul to your spirit. Take your mind, your worries, your thoughts, your will, your choices, your emotions, your pain, your past, and your wounds and submit them to the Healer living inside of you.

If you're ready to do that, confess these words:

God, I submit myself to you now.

Body; submit to my soul.

Soul; submit to my spirit.

Spirit; submit to the Spirit of the living God, and no other.

I want to be preserved complete, without blame, kept in perfect peace.

Amen.

When you're done, write your experience below.

_____

_____

_____

_____

_____

_____

_____

_____

_____

Day 3: Fillers

Read 'Fillers' on pages 76-80, and 'Escape Hatches' and 'What are your favorite means of escape' on page 83-84

If you're in Christ, you're filled with a love that's never going away based on your behavior. Love lives inside your heart because of *grace*. This is the beauty of Christianity and what sets it apart from other religions. We can't save ourselves. We can't heal ourselves. We can't fix ourselves—we have to surrender to the One who does it for us, forgiving us, restoring us, and transforming us—all while we *believe*.

If you believe in Jesus and He lives in you, or if you want this love to live inside your heart forever, making you clean and new, forgiving everything you've ever done and reuniting you with the Love you were created for, then all you have to do is ask! **If you've asked Him to make His home inside of you, write LOVE in the love bucket of your heart.**

No matter how you feel, no matter what you do, and no matter what you believe, you can *never be separated from this love again.*

And I am convinced that nothing can ever separate us from God's love. Neither death nor life, neither angels nor demons, neither our fears for today nor our worries about tomorrow—not even the powers of hell can separate us from God's love. No power in the sky above or in the earth below—indeed, nothing in all creation will ever be able to separate us from the love of God that is revealed in Christ Jesus our Lord. Romans 8:38-39 (NLT)

If your heart is filled with the love of Jesus Christ, then the solution to every one of your problems *already lives inside of you*. Your heart has been made into a new creation

where your old, sinful nature has been crucified; you've been filled, forgiven, and given a new nature! The problem is, if you've been wounded over the course of your life, you probably still remember your old pain.

The heart has been made whole—but it also remembers the pain of the past.

If you're new in Christ but your heart still feels wounded from the pain of the past, write out what you think caused the holes. How do you think your heart looks? What shape is it in?

_____

_____

_____

_____

_____

_____

_____

HOW I FEEL

For as he thinks within himself, so he is.
Proverbs 23:7 (NASB)

Do you remember the Disney movie *The Ugly Dachshund*? A giant Great Dane was raised with a litter of tiny Dachshunds, and the problem was, he thought he was a Dachshund, too! He crawled like a little Dachshund, acted like them, played like them. He didn't realize that he was massive, so he acted small.

Just because he believed he was a Dachshund didn't change the fact that he was a Great Dane.

And just because you believe you're damaged from the past doesn't change the fact that you've been made new in Christ.

If you're in Christ, your heart is a new creation. But you won't act new if you still believe you're crippled. And that's what pain does—it cripples us from seeing the truth of all Christ has made available to us.

How do you see yourself? Take a minute and draw the condition of your love bucket below. Then see how it compares to the truth.

I felt like damaged goods, but I wasn't. I couldn't see the truth as long as the pain went unhealed.

The pain in my love bucket was a hungry monster and always needed to be numbed, silenced, or covered up. **Take a moment and check which 'fillers' you use (or have used) to try and silence, numb, or escape the pain in your love bucket.**

- [ ] DRUGS
- [ ] ALCOHOL
- [ ] OVEREATING
- [ ] RESTRICTING FOOD
- [ ] CIGARETTES
- [ ] SEX

- [ ] OVERACHIEVING
- [ ] PERFECTIONISM
- [ ] INTERNET
- [ ] ESCAPISM
- [ ] WORKING OUT
- [ ] READING

- [ ] CUTTING
- [ ] PORNOGRAPHY
- [ ] SHOPPING
- [ ] _____
- [ ] _____
- [ ] _____

How long have these 'fillers' been used to deal with your pain? Are you tired of them? Do you feel like they control you, or do you control them?

_____

_____

_____

I have a feeling these fillers might numb the pain but don't fix the problem. Are you ready to get rid of these temporary fillers and find a permanent solution?

_____

_____

_____

If you've run to substances, behaviors, relationships, or success to deal with the pain in your heart, it's time to stop running. The pain won't just take care of itself. But I know someone who wants to take the pain for you.

Thank you, Jesus, that You promise to bind up the broken hearted and proclaim freedom for the prisoners. Thank you, Jesus, that You've made me a new creation. Thank you that You want my heart to believe all You've done—and You're going to do a work in me that I cannot do myself. I hand the love bucket of my heart over to You now, asking You to take all my 'fillers.' I'm tired of being filled with something other than You. Fill me again, pour Your love deep inside, and let the medicine of Your presence go deep to every wound, restoring what's been broken. Amen.

Day 4: There's Always a Reason

Read 'There's Always A Reason' on pages 80-82 and 'What Are The Roots Behind These Behaviors' on pages 84-85.

Before you throw a stone of judgment when you see an abusive parent, take a moment and ask *why?* I guarantee you, there's a stack of reasons that you'll never understand behind someone getting to the depraved point where they're able to hurt a child.

And it always involves a broken heart.

When you see a murderer, before you judge take a second. Look through grace, and ask *why?* I promise, there's a lifetime of pain and death behind someone getting to the point where they can callously take life.

And it always involves a broken heart.

That's why, beautiful friend, Jesus is the solution to the world's behavioral problems. His primary mission wasn't to simply come give us a ticket to heaven someday or make us obedient to a bunch of rules. It was to heal the pain in our hearts and make us whole, filling us with Love and changing us from the inside out. He really is the solution for the world—to poverty, abuse, murder, rape, kidnapping, bullying, anger, terrorism, and hate. He takes our broken hearts, heals them, and then we behave differently—not because we're trying to change—but because we submit ourselves to a love that transforms us.

> *After all it is God's approval and not man's impression that matters most. Man sees skin-deep; God knows the heart. Romans 2:29* (The Mirror Bible)

God doesn't just look at your cheating, lying, addiction, depression, anger, slander, gossip, jealousy, and insecurity. He looks at your heart. He can see all the reasons *why you behave the way you do.*

Have you been guilty of looking at the action and not what's behind the action? Maybe someone annoys you and you haven't stopped to ask why. Maybe you're a judgmental person and throw stones instead of offering help. After reading *There's Always A Reason*, write your thoughts below.

_____

_____

_____

For every filler you uncovered in the last chapter, there's always a reason behind it. For every secret food binge, judgmental comment, cheating rendezvous, and drunken downward spiral, there's always pain at the root. Don't kid yourself—you don't just 'dabble' in destructive behaviors. You might not be a slave to addiction, but that doesn't mean you're not in bondage. Pain cries out and must be silenced, and most of the time, we don't know how to run to the Healer.

So we run to a quick fix.

Remember our tree from the last chapter? Let's review the parts of our tree and add **fruit** to the branches. Let's go back to the story in Chapter 2 of *God Loves Ugly* where I stumbled onto late night pornography down at a friend's house.

SEED: The painful experience of pornography as a child planted a seed of shame inside the fertile soil of my heart.

ROOTS: And as I watered the seed of the sexual perversion by thinking shameful thoughts, a root system began to grow.

TRUNK: The shameful thoughts grew into shameful beliefs, and a trunk began to appear from the ground.

BRANCHES: The more I thought and believed I was shameful, the more I felt shameful. The branches of shameful emotions grew everywhere.

BAD FRUIT: And because I felt shameful, I acted that way, numbing the shame with food, alcohol, drugs, and performance.

You see, there's always a reason behind your behaviors, which is why simply trying to change your behavior never really works. Let's take a minute and find out what the reasons are behind your behaviors.

Go back to your list of 'fillers' in the last lesson. These are the bad fruit of your life that you want to cut off your tree. Write out each fruit in the spaces below, and then work backwards until you get to the root.

BAD FRUIT / BEHAVIORS

1.

2.

3.

ROOTS / THOUGHTS

1.

2.

3.

BRANCHES / EMOTIONS

1.

2.

3.

SEEDS / EXPERIENCE

1.

2.

3.

TRUNK / BELIEFS

1.

2.

3.

Hold onto this list. You're going to need it again at the end of the next chapter. You're digging into the soil of your heart with the Master Gardener, doing amazing work to till the soil and bring the pain to the surface. The only reason pain needs to be uncovered is for the purpose of healing it, restoring it, and setting you free.

And you deserve freedom and peace. In fact, you were made for it.

Thank you, Jesus that You've come to heal the painful roots in our heart! And when You heal, we naturally change. We submit ourselves to Your healing medicine, Jesus, and need it in abundant supply! We won't go after behavior modification—it doesn't work. We'll let You go to the root of the pain, healing and breathing life. There's no pain too big for You—and we hand our hearts to You again. Have Your way in us, Father. Amen.

Day 5: Progress Check

If you've made it this far in the workbook, I'm so proud of you! You're doing amazing heart work, uncovering the lies, and beginning to see the solution. And His name is Jesus! His truth really does set our hearts free *where we start acting free!*

Hopefully every day, you've been declaring your lists of new beliefs from Chapter 1, and reversing your word daggers from Chapter 2 with the truth, tilling the soil of your heart. Today, I want you to take a minute and reflect on the changes that have happened in your heart and life since you began this journey.

Your old negative thoughts led to negative beliefs, emotions, and then actions.

NEGATIVE — EXPERIENCES/WORDS — THOUGHTS — BELIEFS — EMOTIONS — ACTIONS

Take a moment and chart how your new declarations have created new thoughts, beliefs, emotions, and behaviors in your life.

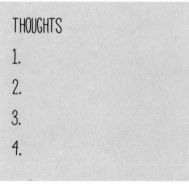

POSITIVE — EXPERIENCES/WORDS — THOUGHTS — BELIEFS — EMOTIONS — ACTIONS

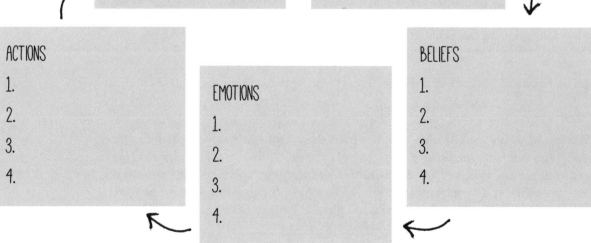

EXPERIENCES / WORDS
1.
2.
3.
4.

THOUGHTS
1.
2.
3.
4.

ACTIONS
1.
2.
3.
4.

EMOTIONS
1.
2.
3.
4.

BELIEFS
1.
2.
3.
4.

It's encouraging to see how putting truth inside your heart begins to heal and change your life! It might not happen overnight—remember, some of you have had decades believing, watering, and partnering with lies—but the more you water the truth, the more that truth will begin to bloom in your heart!

Your broken heart can be healed. Completely. It's your inheritance in Christ! The journey towards whole-hearted living doesn't have to be arduous, especially since you never have to walk it alone.

> *"So be strong and courageous! Do not be afraid and do not panic before them. For the LORD your God will personally go ahead of you. He will neither fail you nor abandon you." Deuteronomy 31:6* (NLT)

God doesn't demand perfection. In fact, He has so much grace for you on this journey of healing. He simply wants to be the hand you hold as you walk into all He has for you—with relationship being the prize. Have grace for yourself as you heal—God has it for you. He died so you could have it.

Take a moment and write a prayer of grace for yourself, letting you off the hook for not being perfect in the process of healing. Let go of your own expectations to be further along than you are. You only have grace for *today*, and that's it. Wherever you are is exactly where you need to be—not further along, not better, not acting freer, and definitely not perfect. You just have to be willing to go on an adventure with the King, and He'll get you to your destination.

Write your prayer of grace to yourself below.

_____

_____

_____

_____

Thank you, Jesus, for the journey You've walked with us so far. We're exactly where we need to be, and You have so much grace for us as we walk into Your Promised Land of freedom. We receive this grace, asking it to light the path as we continue our adventure together.

We trust You, Jesus. Thank you for caring about our hearts. You take such good care of us. Amen.

Week 5: **GROUP DISCUSSION QUESTIONS**

Chapter 4: There's Always a Reason

1 **Begin with a prayer, committing to Ephesians 3:20, that God will do "Exceedingly, abundantly above all you could ask or think."**

2 **Read the 'We Believe God Can' list aloud.** Set your hope on God exceeding your imagination, not on your own limitations. Briefly give any testimony of your declarations blooming to life over the past week.

3 **Discussion Questions:**
• Did you speak your two declaration lists over the last week? Is it getting easier? Share any breakthroughs that occurred.

• Discuss the concept of *'Spirit, Soul, Body'* and the differences between each part. What part of you carries the most weight? What do you focus on the most? Does your focus need to shift?

• If your soul has been wounded, what 'fillers' have you turned to over the years to numb and appease a heart in pain?

• Have you lived in shame and condemnation for running to things that hurt and destroyed you?

• We always want the fruit of our lives to change, sometimes ignoring the root. In reading this chapter, did you discover roots in your heart that are causing bad fruit?

• Are you able to have more grace for yourself and those around you after realizing that there's always a reason behind every behavior?

• Put on the new lens of grace. What's one thing you're committing to see differently about yourself—maybe your food addiction, lying, jealousy or people pleasing? Have grace for yourself as you allow healing deep down into the roots. Grace precedes change.

4 **Close with a prayer, declaring that God will fulfill His promise of freedom for every heart.**

5 **Have *Chapter 5* and the assignments completed by the next time you meet. (Pages 86-108)**

week six
Chapter 5 Jesus / Steve

Day 1: The Ugly Truth

Read pages 89-94 in *God Loves Ugly*.

Jesus.

Even the mention of that name sends butterflies fluttering deep inside my heart. This man—this man who looked at me with affection while at the bottom of a dungeon—tear stained, bruised, bloody, and broken. This man who crawled into my ugly pain *with* me and wrapped His arms around my brokenness, committing to stay there forever—*even if I never changed.* This man who never judged with condemnation at the girl I had become, but always believed with grace at the woman I was destined to be. This man who loved me even when I was destructive, angry, and abusive.

But who also loved me enough not to let me stay that way.

This man is my best friend Jesus. And for the life of me, I can't figure out why the whole world doesn't run into His arms full of intoxicating Love.

Unfortunately, there's been a big difference between the Jesus that I've actually experienced and the Jesus that's been portrayed to the world through mainstream religion. So many horrific things have been done in Jesus' name over the centuries that I know He had nothing to do with. The world doesn't read their Bibles—but they do read their Christians. And most of the time, Christians are the biggest reason why people don't want our Jesus.

Over the years, followers of Jesus have been mean, judgmental, pious, and exclusive. They've tended to throw stones of accusation and condemnation. But their abusive actions weren't representative of my Jesus. He was the kindest, most graceful, approachable, accepting person to ever walk the earth. And He was the perfect depiction of the heart of Father God.

What Jesus have you encountered over the course of your life? Has He been a shaming, cruel, taskmaster? Has He been portrayed to make you feel guilty, unworthy, and lacking? Or has your Jesus been the kind, loving, accepting man I described above?

Write out an honest description of your personal Jesus below.

_____

_____

_____

Years ago, I toured with an artist who had a very cranky, grumpy, demanding and sometimes mean production manager who was in charge of overseeing the set up of all the gear, lights, and sound for the concert. He would huff around cussing and yelling at the local church crew, always frustrated that things weren't being done perfectly. And because this person was representing the artist playing that night, at times, the church staff where we played got a bad taste in their mouth for the whole operation after encountering the grumpy production manager. But several times, I heard people talking after they had met the actual artist whose name was on the bill. They were surprised that the talent was nothing like the man he employed to set up the show.

There are a lot of grumpy, mean, demanding Christians setting up shows for Jesus. But just because they act that way, it doesn't mean Jesus does.

Is your perception of Jesus from your encounters with Him and from who He is in scripture, or is it from encountering His followers? Could your perception be tainted if you've had bad experiences with church, religion, or Christians in the past? Is He still getting the blame for things He had nothing to do with? Write your experiences and thoughts below.

_____

_____

_____

I Corinthians 13 is the LOVE chapter. If God is LOVE and Jesus is His earthly representation on the earth, let's see who this God and Jesus really are based upon this scripture in verses 4-8.

"Love is patient and kind; love is not jealous or boastful; it is not arrogant or rude. Love does not insist on its own way; it is not irritable or resentful; it does not rejoice at wrong, but rejoices in the right. Love bears all things, believes all things, hopes all things, endures all things. Love never ends"

Now, let's go back and insert the names Jesus & God for LOVE to find out exactly who they are.

_____ *are patience and kind.*

_____ *are not jealous or boastful.*

_____ *are not arrogant or rude.*

_____ *do not insist on their own way.*

_____ *are not irritable or resentful.*

_____ *do not rejoice at wrong, but rejoice in the right.*

_____ *bears all things, believe all things, hopes all things, endures all things.*

_____ *never ends.*

If this description is the Jesus you've experienced, then you're on the right track. But if it's far from the Jesus you've encountered, it might be time to go to Him as your primary source—instead of His followers.

In no way am I saying you shouldn't be part of a body of believers. The church was God's idea, and believe me, you want to be a part of the organization that the gates of hell cannot prevail against! (Matthew 16:18) What I am saying, however, is that you have to let the actual Jesus define your definition of Him—and not what religion, churches, and followers of Christ might have portrayed.

A lot of times, we get angry at Jesus when we're really just hurt by people who say they represent Him.

In *The Ugly Truth* on pages 92-94, God was seen as distant and far off in my childhood, looming overhead in condemnation, waiting to zap anyone who failed to obey. But instead of God having us under a microscope, waiting for us to fail, as I once believed, scripture proves He's a bit different.

> *"For all the promises of God find their Yes in him. That is why it is through him that we utter our Amen to God for his glory." 2 Corinthians 1:20* (ESV)

The promises of God are **'Yes and Amen!'** Instead of God hoping for us to fail, he's actually equipped us to succeed through all He's made available in Christ! God wants you to win, and He's already won the victory for you!

Does your Jesus and your God operate more in the realm of failure, rules, and judgment with 'shouldn'ts and couldn'ts'? Or does your God feel abundant with possibility with 'yes and amen?' Do you feel like He's holding obedience over your head, or empowering you to destiny?

_____

_____

_____

The Jesus I saw growing up as a preacher's kid involved a lot of church politics. There were a lot shameful looks; church splits over things like drums, and a separation of the "good people" from the "bad" based upon behavior. This Jesus wasn't someone I wanted much to do with, especially since I couldn't measure up to Christianity's standard of perfection while being in so much pain. So I did the only thing I knew to do.

I rebelled and I ran.

Have you run from Jesus, like I did, because you feel like you can't be enough for Him? Have you run because He seems cruel, judgmental, and demanding? Do you avoid diving all the way into the Jesus pool because it feels too overwhelming—and you know you'll never measure up? Explain any running you might have done below.

_____

_____

_____

_____

Maybe you're not rebellious, and on the outside you're not running. You go to church, you read your bible, you pray. But maybe you distrust Him because He seems to have disappointed you. Maybe you won't give Him your entire heart because you've been disappointed in the past. Write any heart running you've done below.

_____

_____

_____

_____

Beautiful friend, if you've run from Jesus because you feel like you're not enough, or because He's cruel and demanding, or because of shame—or even because you think He's let you down—then I have news for you. You haven't run from Jesus—you've run from a false Jesus called _religion_. And I'm proud of you for running.

I'm so thankful I ran from lifeless religion that's worse than a prison cage. Religion is all about rules—but Jesus is all about relationship. Religion is about performance—but Jesus is about wholeness. Religion is about perfectionism—but Jesus is about identity.

If you've run from the false Jesus, it's time for you to run to the real Jesus and see if He's the love He says He is. This Jesus is accepting, kind, loving, and consistent. This Jesus won't leave you, He's come to bind up your broken heart, and proclaim freedom over your life. His plans are to prosper you and not to harm you, to give you a hope and a future. Yes, He tells you the truth, and sometimes the truth hurts, but He never does it with condemnation. He's not consumed with sin—He dealt with sin on the cross! He's obsessed with righteousness. And you just happen to be the righteousness of God in Christ. (2 Corinthians 5:21)

If you're realizing your vision of Jesus might need some fine-tuning, then take a moment and ask Him to show you who He really is.

Out of all your hurts, experiences, and encounters, will the real Jesus please stand up?

Pray this prayer below.

Jesus, I want the real You. I don't want the Jesus that religion has portrayed—a cruel, tasking, shameful man. I don't want the Jesus that brings with Him guilt and condemnation. I want You. I want Your truth to fill my eyes and heart. I want to see the real You, to feel You, to experience You. Come show me who You are. I give You permission to fill my eyes with truth as I turn to You. Amen.

Write any fine-tuning or adjusting you want in your vision below, taking off the old goggles that see a shameful Jesus, and putting on this new Jesus filled with acceptance, grace, and love.

_____

_____

_____

_____

_____

_____

_____

_____

_____

Jesus, give me eyes to see and ears to hear the truth. I'm tired of believing lies—if You're real, I want to know it. If I can see You, I want to see You. If I can hear You, I want to hear You. If Your love is the solution for my pain, then I want it. Amen.

Day 2: Perfectionism vs. Excellence

The desire for perfection results in performance, while the desire for excellence is rooted in identity.

Every person on the planet was created to produce fruit, and believe me, you produce something. A heart that's rooted in love has a harvest of all sorts of excellent, life-giving fruits—year round. But a heart that believes its unlovable will always grow fruit that leads to sin and death.

One of my least favorite fruits that can grow out of a heart believing it's unlovable is the bad fruit of perfectionism. Perfectionism is a nasty monster who's always hungry, always demanding more. It brings with it a plague of dissatisfaction. And nothing is ever good enough.

Perfectionists aren't bad people. They just don't believe they're lovable as they are.

They always need to be more. If they can just become (insert achievement, relationship, status, or appearance), they're convinced that they'll finally be lovable. But if they ever reach their coveted goal, love and acceptance is always contingent on that goal being maintained.

Which means love is always *conditional.*

For years, I thought if I could just fit into a certain pair of jeans I bought while on tour in Switzerland, I'd finally feel beautiful. I dieted, starved myself, worked out incessantly, until one day, I finally got those darn jeans to button over my backside. But instead of feeling beautiful, I noticed my thighs still rubbed up against each other when I walked, and I set off to lose enough weight were I'd have a gap between my legs. After starving myself even more until my thighs didn't touch, I noticed the cellulite. Then after the cellulite was starved away, I needed to work on my splotchy skin. After the splotchy skin, my hair was still straight as a board.

The problem wasn't ever my jean size, skin, cellulite, or flat hair. The problem was a heart filled with self-hatred.

Perfectionists can never be satisfied when they believe they're unlovable. Their vision is consumed with what's wrong, so they always find something wrong. They focus on what's lacking instead of what's already there.

Do you struggle with perfectionism? Do you believe you're lovable as you are, or do you constantly find reasons why you're not?

_____

_____

_____

_____

How has this possible measuring stick of perfectionism played into your relationship with God? Do you believe He only loves you when you act lovable—being sinless, perfect, faithful, and performing acts of service? Is His love for you conditional on your behavior?

_____

_____

_____

_____

The world operates on a conditional love system.

IF you look a certain way, I'll be attracted to you.

IF you stay looking that way, I'll stay married to you.

IF you're a good friend to me, I'll stay friends with you.

IF you have a certain degree, then we'll hire you.

A conditional love system is always contingent on a behavior, an appearance, or a social or economic status being maintained. But that's not the way God works. He works on an unconditional love system where He loved you before you ever did anything wrong and continues to love you even when you do.

> *"For God so loved the world, that he gave his only Son, that whoever believes in him should not perish but have eternal life." John 3:16* (ESV)

God's love for you preceded your salvation. God's love for you started before the earth was ever created. God's love for you was never contingent on your love, service, or need for Him. He loves you regardless—*because He is love.*

Sadly, churches can take on the world's culture of 'conditional love,' training sheep to earn Father's affection through service, works, and obedience. And when you believe God's love for you is contingent on your behaviors, I promise you—you're going to perform.

If your Jesus, your God, or your church has a conditional love culture where performance runs rampant, then I guarantee you, you've had to keep secrets to stay 'loved.' People tend to keep their struggles, bondages, and shortcomings hidden in fear that they might lose their platform, or be seen as less spiritual when perfection is expected.

Have you kept secrets out of shame? Have you hidden your true self and your struggles from your church, friends, or ministry? Have you been ashamed of your addiction, your struggle, or your bondage? Take a moment and write any secrets you've been afraid to reveal in the space below that you've kept hidden out of shame or fear.

_____

_____

_____

_____

When you keep secrets out of shame, believing God or Christian culture won't love you if they see your struggle, you can't ever be completely free. Your secret actually *blocks your heart* from the solution to your problem.

Friends, I don't believe the hardest part about being a Christian is being obedient. I don't think it's about being faithful or serving God. We're really good at performing for love in our performance-driven culture, and it's made its way into our churches. The hardest part about being a Christian is learning to receive a love you know you don't deserve.

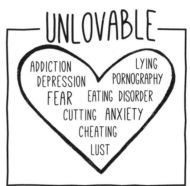

It's hard to let yourself be loved when you believe parts of your life are unlovable.

Take a moment and assess your heart. Yes, you're filled with the love of God if you're in Christ, but do you really believe it? If you believe you're unlovable right now—if you believe you're not enough, or you need to be more for God before He can love you, then I guarantee you, *you're performing*. If you've put yourself in the judgment seat, evaluating your past, your behaviors, and your achievements, then I guarantee you—*you're performing.*

The only way to be free is to simply receive the one thing you can never deserve— and that's the unconditional love of God. It's hard when you know what you've done in the past. It's hard when your track record keeps reminding you how sinful, broken, and screwed up you are. But you can't fix yourself. You can't heal yourself. And you can't make yourself lovable.

You're already lovable because Love chose you.

Take at least ten minutes today and say *yes* to this Love. Ask this Love to go into the cracks of shame, the places you've deemed unlovable. Cry it out, scream, sob—but just say yes. Your mind will race with all the reasons why you *don't* deserve it—but push them aside and say *yes* again.

Say yes right now to this love. Say yes to the love you were made for.

Write your experience, struggles, thoughts, and encounter with Love.

_____

_____

_____

_____

Day 3: **God Loves Ugly**

Read 'God Loves Ugly' and 'Religion V Relationship' on pages 94-103 and 'Who is God To You' and 'Who Do You Believe God Is' on pages 106-107.

I didn't want God. I wanted Love. And the two just happened to be the same thing, as I learned that night long ago in Canada.

After reading about my radical experience with a God that I wasn't looking for, what were your first thoughts? Did you believe me? Did you have moments of doubt, unsure if experiences like that actually happen because they haven't happened to you? Were you jealous of my story, longing for a supernatural touch from God? Write out your raw, honest thoughts about my supernatural experience with God that shifted the course of my life.

_____

_____

_____

_____

Every person has a very different history with God. Some grew up in church, and some didn't. Some grew up in controlling and abusive religious settings, and others had beautiful, life changing encounters. Some grew up with the spiritual realm being normal, and others grew up believing in what they could see with their physical eyes.

What does your history with God look like? Has He seemed distant and far off, a big, robed man in the sky on a throne looking down at the ants that play below? Or has He been so close you could feel His love? Is He scary? Cruel? Have things happened during your life that you can't explain that might have God behind them?

Write out any significant experiences you've had with God over the years. If you haven't had any and are angry or disappointed in God, write that out, too.

_____

_____

_____

_____

Whether your earthly parents were around or not, your mother and father came together, and you were the result. It's difficult to hear of God as Father and not be influenced by our earthly perception of what a father is like because of our own experiences—good and bad.

Was your earthly father distant? Was he loving and kind? Did he make you feel like you hung the moon, or did he ignore and neglect you? Maybe even abuse or abandon you?

Take a moment and write out a description of your earthly father.

_____

_____

_____

How has your experience with an earthly father influenced your perception of God your Father? Have you projected things onto God and expected Him to be a certain way because your earthy dad was that way?

_____

_____

_____

Every baby who has ever been born longs to be loved, held, nurtured and adored. There's a reason why children aren't lining up to be put into orphanages, but the ones orphaned pray for a forever family to finally want them. Remember, you're created in the image of Love, so of course your heart craves it like a watering hole in a scorching desert. You need it to thrive. You need it to come alive. You need it to be made whole—it's in your DNA.

Do you want to be loved more than anything else? Write out the longings of your heart for acceptance, love, and affection below.

_____

_____

_____

How has your longing for love defined your life? How has it ruined your life? Have you made mistakes that you regret while searching for love?

_____

_____

_____

The reason why salvation is so brilliant is because it becomes the solution for every problem you face. God made your heart to long for love, and when you choose Him, *Love makes His home inside your heart forever.* When you're filled with Jesus, you're filled with love, you're broken heart is restored, your wounds are healed, your sins are forgiven, and you're forever connected with the God who created you.

Most people have a radical salvation encounter, experiencing the love of God at the moment of convergence. It's a powerful mystery when the presence of Love comes to tabernacle inside of you, filling you to overflowing. But after that happens, your memories of the past remain. *You remember that you're not lovable* as evidenced by your past, the world around you, and imperfect people.

So instead of continuing to run back to the relationship we can have with this Love, a lot of times, we move into the 'unworthy zone' where we stop experiencing His affection and start trying to earn it.

Do you know you're saved and that God loves you, but you still struggle with feeling unworthy? Does this belief make you run to God when you're struggling, or away from Him?

_____

_____

_____

Dear friend, you will approach God in the way you perceive Him.

If you believe He expects you to be perfect, then you'll only come to Him when you feel sinless. If you believe He's untrustworthy, then you'll keep Him at an arms length. If you believe He takes you as you are—ugly, bruised and bleeding—then you'll run to Him all the time.

Your perception of God determines what God you encounter.

After reading *Who Do You Believe God Is* on page 106-107, take a moment and make the most important list of your life.

Who is this God to you? Who do you believe Him to be? What are His characteristics, His tendencies, and His personality traits? What do you believe His will is—do you believe He's really good with so much pain in your life? (And don't write down what you think you're *supposed* to write about God. Don't write down He's loving if you truly believe He hasn't loved you well. Don't write down that He's faithful if you think He's let you down. This is your opportunity to write down what you really think! He's not going to strike you down for getting honest; in fact, He's been waiting for you to get there).

Take a good hunk of time and write out a thorough description of your perception of God.

_____

_____

_____

_____

_____

_____

_____

_____

_____

_____

_____

_____

_____

_____

_____

_____

_____

_____

Day 4: First Loved

Read 'Love Deficiency' on pages 103-105.

Take a moment and think about the worst thing you've ever done, or that's ever been done to you. Maybe your mind goes to that time in the backseat of that car, or that time in the abortion clinic. Maybe it's when you were being abused, or when you were the one abusing. Maybe your head is filled with thoughts of bingeing, pornography, cutting, cheating, adultery, or promiscuity. More than likely, your head and heart burst with shame and you lower your head—cringing at a past that you can never erase.

Now, take the things that stuck out the most, and write them on the bucket to the right.

At your worst, most disgusting, most fragile, most shameful moment of existence, there is a God who looked at you with the same affection that He looked at you with on the day you were born. There is a God who never flinched, never faltered, never wavered in His affection for you.

There is a God who was never ashamed of you.

Rewrite your shame in the bucket below that's surrounded, filled, and covered in God's love.

Take a moment and soak in the revelation that your shame has never made you unlovable. Your God has never been ashamed of you—and He's never not loved you. Meditate on that reality and write your feelings and thoughts below.

_____

_____

_____

_____

A lot of us put 'love' and 'approval' in the same camp, but they're two entirely different things. God didn't approve of me stealing all throughout high school, but not for one second was He ashamed of me. He knew I was stealing out of pain and that I needed His love. God didn't approve of the destructive behaviors of addiction, but He never looked at me with condemnation. He knew I was trying to numb the pain that only He could fix. God didn't approve of the boy who abused me, but He never stopped loving me. *And He never stopped loving that boy, even while he was sexually abusing a child.*

Love and approval are not the same thing.

If my son Moses grows up to be a meth addict who goes on a murdering spree, I would never approve of his actions. But I would never stop loving my son—no matter what he had done.

Have you had 'love' and 'approval' in the same category? Have you believed that God could only love you if He approved of your life, your past, and your behaviors? Write your thoughts below.

_____

_____

_____

God's love for you has never been contingent on your behavior—otherwise, it wouldn't be unconditional. His love is the most constant thing in the entire universe, and that love, beautiful friend, is always pointed straight at you. You can't run from it. You can't get away from it. He loves you whether or not you want to be loved.

But it's entirely up to you whether or not you receive it.

I John 4:19 says *We love because He **first** loved us.* (NIV) This means that your ability to love is actually contingent on your ability to *be loved first.*

Have you had a hard time loving yourself, loving others, and loving God because you believed you weren't lovable?

_____

_____

_____

Have you been trying to love God, worship Him, and live for Him, but it feels like striving and effort?

_____

_____

_____

If you're not very fond of yourself, then you need to let Him love you _first_. If you find it hard to love others, then you need to let Him love you _first_. If you find it hard to love God, then take two steps back, and let Him love you _first_.

You can only give away whatever it is that you've allowed yourself to receive. So if you're having a hard time loving, then you probably haven't received the truth until it's transformed you.

In the space below, write out five areas of your life that you don't believe are lovable. Meditate on God's unconditional love being poured OVER those areas of your life. Close your eyes and see the liquid love of God going into the cracks of your shame, covering, surrounding, and invading the things that you've hated about yourself. See His first love engulfing your abuse, your behaviors, your body, and your past. See His first love that never ceases, never hesitates, and never stops.

Write what you see, feel, and hear in the spaces below.

LOVE

LOVE

LOVE

Day 5: Experiencing God

Read 'Ask Him To Show Up, Right Here, Right Now' on pages 107-108.

As a preacher's kid, I grew up knowing all about God.

I could quote scriptures, I could tell Bible stories—I'd even tell you that 'God loves you' while believing that there was no way He could love terrible ole me. But just because my head was filled with the knowledge of God didn't mean my heart believed that information.

Can you give one example of something that you know in your head, but don't believe in your heart? (You will know you believe it because you'll act like it!)

_____

_____

_____

There is a very real difference between what you know in your head and what you believe in your heart, and one that must be differentiated inside the realm of your relationship with God. God isn't a theory or debate, or a sermon or teaching. _He's a person to know and experience._

He didn't tear the veil, ask you to approach His throne with boldness and confidence, seat you in heavenly places, and come live inside your heart so that you could simply learn about Him. He wants to know you and be known by you.

He wants you to experience Him.

If you spend all your time as a Christian listening to a preacher talk about God, or simply read about Him but don't make space to just be with Him—then you might know _about Him_ without _knowing Him._ When you encounter His presence, hearing His whispers and building relationship, you have an actual, life-giving, organic friendship, relationship, and romance with God.

Would you say you know about God, or would you say you know Him?

_____

_____

_____

My head knowledge about God didn't make me behave differently. I lived as an unlovable, shameful blob of matter for decades even though my head was filled with the truth. My experiences with Him were what changed my life. The more I began encountering God's love through worship, intimacy, prayer, soaking, waiting, and meditation, the more my heart believed. The more He touched my pain, healing me from the inside out, the easier it was to believe.

And you behave according to what you believe.

Do you want to believe but don't know how? Do you feel like you know but don't know how to get that information down into your heart? Write any frustrations you have with your head knowledge below.

_____

_____

_____

The left side of your brain is like a filing cabinet, retaining all sorts of autobiographical memories. And out of those memories and experiences, you formulate rational, reasoning thoughts with logic and explanations. *Once you form this logical thinking, it's extremely resistant to change.*

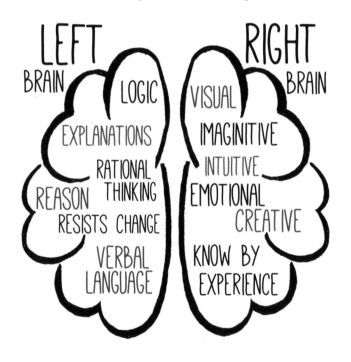

For example, this left side of your brain learns about a cat by reading about cats, or being told about them. It learns cognitively through words and language, stories and descriptions. But the right brain learns about cats by experiencing them—by petting a kitten, hearing their purrs, and feeling their bite. The right side of the brain is the seat of our emotions—its creative, visual, imaginative, and intuitive. It knows things because it experiences them.

Say you broke your leg and were stuck in a cast while it healed. If you grew up learning that God doesn't heal people and you'd never actually seen anyone healed, you might not believe me if I told you God wanted to heal your leg.

Remember, your logical thinking is extremely resistant to change.

But if you let me lay hands on your leg and pray, and that leg was miraculously put back together in an instant, your experience with healing would make it easy for you to believe God still heals.

Experience makes it easy to believe.

That's why just learning about God doesn't really change our behaviors. In order to really change your behaviors, *you need an encounter.*

God created both sides of our brains, and we need to encounter Him with both.

Do you feel like you approach God more from your left brain—through logic, reason, and explanations? Or do you feel like you approach God more from your right brain—through emotions, feelings, and experiences?

_____

_____

_____

Reread pages 107-108 and ask God to show up right here, right now.

Go somewhere alone. Get away from distractions, turn on music without words or worship music, and quiet your mind. If this is hard for you, your logical mind will go crazy, trying to shut down your heart. But don't let it win. If God is real, then He wants to be with you. If God is love, then He wants to love you. If God is compassionate, then He wants to heal you.

Give Him space to do it. Ask Him to show up. Ask Him to reveal His presence.

Pray this prayer:

Father, show me who You are. Show me a real, powerful, encounter with You—with Your love and Your presence. I can't keep living for a God I know about, I need a God that I can be with, encountering, talking to, hearing from, and being healed by. I'm through with lifeless Christianity that demands I follow rules without relationship. I want relationship right now. I want YOU.

Close your eyes and see the love bucket of your heart. I want to see Jesus walk up in front of you with kindness in His eyes. See His gaze that's fixed on you. See His compassion, His mercy, His tenderness and His love. See the holes in His hands and feet where He bled for you—where He bought your freedom. See His smile, the smile that believes in you, that's not ashamed of you, that's not angry with you. See this Jesus, and hand Him your heart—whatever state that heart is in. It might be full of word daggers. It might be crippled by pain. It might be burdened with addiction and depression. Just give it to Him and say *Yes.*

Take the list of wounded roots you made at the end of the last chapter in Lesson 25 and bring it before Him. Ask Him about the roots, letting Him pour His love into each place of brokenness. Ask Him to pour in His love to kick out your fear, to displace your shame.

What does Jesus feel like?
What does Jesus look like?
What does Jesus smell like?
What does His voice sound like?

Drink in each moment with your Savior.

After you've spent time with this beautiful Jesus, write your experience below.

_____

_____

_____

_____

_____

_____

_____

_____

_____

_____

_____

Week 6: GROUP DISCUSSION QUESTIONS

Chapter 5: Jesus / Steve

1 **Begin with a prayer, thanking God that absolutely nothing you've ever done can separate you from His love. (Romans 8:38-39)**

2 **Read the 'We Believe God Can' list aloud.** Set your hope on God's love healing you, restoring you, and bringing new life. Briefly give any testimony of your declarations blooming to life over the past week.

3 **Discussion Questions:**
• Has everyone been declaring the truth? What's one perception that's changed since you've started this process?

• What is your view of Jesus? Of God? Of the Holy Spirit? Are they distant, judgmental and cruel, or close, loving and kind?

• What experiences helped shape your perception of God? (earthly father, church, Christians, men, media, etc). Is your view incorrect?

• According to Romans 8:38, nothing can separate us from the love of God. Read this verse again. Have you believed the lie that your sin makes God angry, ashamed, or that He withholds His love?

• Do you believe something you've done has made you unworthy of His love?

• Have you struggled with perfectionism and performance in your relationship with God, trying to be worthy of His affection?

• The church sometimes teaches people to love God instead of receiving love from Him. I John 4:19 says "We love him because He first loved us." Have you been trying to love God before you've received love from Him?

• Are you striving to earn His unconditional love when it's free?

• So many times, we love to learn *about* God, yet in relationship, He created us to actually *experience* Him. When you asked Him to show up and love you, what happened?

4 **Close with a prayer, declaring that God has never left you, and He will never forsake you.**

5 **Have *Chapter 6* and the assignments completed by the next time you meet. (Pages 110-130)**

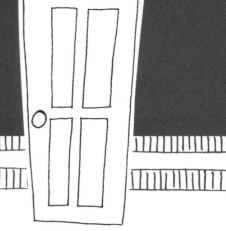

week seven
Chapter 6 Monsters
Chapter 7 40 Days and a Horse

Day 1: **Cycles of Shame**

Read 'God Loves Ugly' on pages 113-118.

Behind every controlling behavior is a foundation of shame. Always.

After my radical encounter with God that night in Canada, I made a 180 degree turn and went from being an insecure druggie to a Jesus freak in an instant. The truth was, I had encountered the real Jesus and wanted to live my life staying as close to His presence and His love as I possibly could. But even though my heart had been fully saved, freed, and redeemed, it still remembered all the pain from my past.

And those memories carried with them mountains of shame.

I wanted to be zapped into wholeness the second I said yes to Jesus. I wanted to be completely transformed and perfect—never struggling again. But I found out very quickly, salvation might be instant, but working out that salvation involves a lot of fear and trembling. (Philippians 2:12)

The shame of my past led me to spiritual performance and striving. The shame that I was still struggling with as a Christian led to fear of letting God and others down, which led to more hiding, which led to even more shame. Shame leads to fear, fear leads to control, and controlling behaviors always lead to more shame. The cycle continues until the shame *loses its power*.

If you have any controlling behaviors in your life, have you ever thought about shame being behind those behaviors?

_____

_____

Years ago if I passed a Louis Vuitton store, I was always too ashamed to step inside. I was ashamed that my clothes weren't expensive enough, and that my handbag wasn't up to their standard. I knew I didn't have the money to buy anything and felt like the salespeople would be able to read the 'middle class' stamp across my forehead, be rude, turn me away, and wonder why I thought myself good enough to come inside in the first place.

Deep down, this is exactly how I felt about my new salvation experience. I looked through the window of shame at all Jesus offered in the realm of blessing, forgiveness, freedom, redemption and felt completely unworthy to set foot inside with my track record of struggles. I'd look down at my tattered soul, still imperfect. I'd look down at my current addictions and bondages, and shame would keep me from stepping inside my inheritance. The shame would keep me in fear, afraid God and His followers wouldn't love me, which led to all sorts of controlling behaviors to try and cover up.

Have you ever felt this way about salvation—that you needed to clean yourself up before deserving all that Christ freely gives?

_____

_____

_____

Do you struggle with shame from your past? Are you ashamed that you're not further along, thinner, smarter, or more successful? Are you ashamed that you still struggle with things that you think you should be free from? Take a moment, get quiet, and write out your honest struggles with the monster of shame.

_____

_____

_____

_____

Does this shame lead to fear in your life? Fear of being rejected? Fear of being hurt? Fear of being worthy? Write out any fear produced from your shame.

_____

_____

_____

When shame and fear are present, there will always be an action produced. My shame manifested in the control of food, the control of people, and a stressful micro-manager who was petrified of failure.

Has your shame and fear produced controlling behaviors in your life? Do you control your husband, your children, your friends? Or does it manifest in the form of material things like food, substances, money, jobs, hobbies, or achievement?

_____

_____

_____

_____

_____

The first time shame entered the world was back in Genesis 3. Adam and Eve had eaten from the tree of the knowledge of good and evil, opening their eyes to their nakedness. As a result, they covered themselves out of shame. When they realized they were exposed, naked, and seen, they sewed fig leaves together to hide their exposure from God.

Dear friends, nothing has changed.

When we partner with shame, in any capacity as believers, we cover ourselves and hide from God.

When you experience shame, do you see how you hide yourself from God? Do you like to feel worthy of His love before you allow yourself to receive it? Take a moment and write out how you might run from God and cover yourself if you feel ashamed.

_____

_____

_____

Have you ever thought about why Adam and Eve chose their loins as their 'shameful parts?' Why weren't they ashamed of their feet, or maybe their shoulders? Why did they cover up their loins out of shame?

_____

_____

_____

The loins are the place that God created for intimacy. The loins are the place that God created for two people to come together in nakedness, and *life is created out of that love.*

You were created to be naked and exposed to love.

And out of that exposure to love, life is created.

The reason why the enemy wants us to cover ourselves in shame out of unworthiness is because he knows that shame cuts you off from the source of love. If you stay ashamed of yourself, in any way, you block yourself from the oneness, intimacy, and love you need to create life.

We won't go into a birds and the bees talk here, but intimacy can't happen when you're covered. You must be exposed to become one with love.

Take a moment and think about shame blocking the creation of life. When you block yourself from being fully seen out of shame and unworthiness, what is produced from your shame? Is it good fruit or bad fruit? Name several examples.

_____

_____

_____

When I would do something as a Christian that I was ashamed of or that I thought made me unworthy, I would either run, or try to clean myself off before I felt worthy to come back to God.

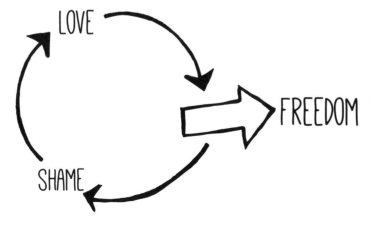

But that's not how love works. Let's see what happens to the Shame—Fear—Control cycle if after shame happens, it stays uncovered and brought immediately to love.

If you immediately introduce the shame of your binge, your cheating, your lying, your pornography, your gossip to God and allow yourself to be loved *as you are*, **fear of rejection can never enter the picture.** You cut it off before it has a chance to produce controlling behaviors.

Take ten minutes and uncover your shame before God. If the shame of your past or present behaviors is leading to fear of rejection, then I know you have behaviors in your life that you wish weren't there. *It's time to get off this vicious cycle.* And it starts with uncovering your shame and exposing it to unconditional love.

Close your eyes for a while. See how you may have covered up abuse with performance, inadequacy with addiction, or sins with rebellion or performance. Whatever it is that you're ashamed of, I want you to see yourself taking off the things you've used to hide that shame, and then *let your shame be loved.* Watch Father pouring in His affection, watch Jesus holding on and never letting go. Feel the Holy Spirit filling you from the inside out with a love that's never been ashamed of you.

After you've had an encounter with the God who delivers us from our shame and gives us a double portion, write your experience below.

_____

_____

_____

_____

_____

_____

_____

"So now there is no condemnation for those who belong to Christ Jesus." Romans 8:1 (NLT)

"Instead of your shame you will receive a double portion, and instead of disgrace you will rejoice in your inheritance. And so you will inherit a double portion in your land, and everlasting joy will be yours." Isaiah 61:7 (NIV)

Day 2: **Black & White**

Read pages 118-130 in *God Loves Ugly*, **completing Chapter 6.**

Good or bad, black or white. If you've struggled with perfectionism, performance, insecurity or self-hatred, there's a good chance that you're an extremist, in some ways, like I am. This characteristic isn't necessarily a bad thing since it's the way God created us. When I get into something, I'm all in, which is a fabulous character trait—especially when you're a Christian. But your greatest strength can become your greatest weakness if it's overextended and unhealed.

And that's a lesson I learned the hard way.

After reading about my extremes with food, bouncing from overeating to anorexia, then to bulimia, then overeating again, could you relate to my struggles? Or have you had other extremes in your life that have been very black and white, right or wrong? Have you found yourself on a downward spiral? (Performance, drugs, cutting, lying, cheating, pornography, etc.)

_____

_____

_____

Our physical bodies bear the brunt of the pain in our hearts—housing that pain and then walking around with it. And when our hearts carry unhealed pain, we take it out on our bodies, even though our bodies have little to do with the problem.

Do you take the pain in your heart out on your body? Are you a slave to exercise, perfection, food, work, cutting, pornography, sex, etc? Write down any ways you beat up your body to try and numb the pain in your heart.

_____

_____

_____

_____

_____

My obsession with my body wasn't really about my physical frame. I hated what was *inside* so nothing was ever good enough on the *outside*. Eating disorders or food addictions, as well as sins against the body, are just ways to beat up on yourself a little more. At the end of the day, you're just giving yourself what you think you deserve.

When you want love more than anything but you don't think you deserve it, you flog yourself up for not being worthy of what you desire.

I've noticed in my own life, if I don't get an obsessive thought under control in about ninety seconds, it starts to take over and control me. Have you noticed thoughts that have led to obsessions that consume your emotions, thoughts, and vision?

Write out any obsessions that take you away from peace, love, joy, and freedom.

_____

_____

_____

_____

In the last lesson, we talked about the Shame—Fear—Control cycle and how it plays into destructive behaviors that repeat like a broken record. But when shame is immediately brought to love, love heals and behaviors are changed. The one thing that's necessary in order to run to God when shame comes calling is the one thing only Christ can give:

Grace.

What is your description of God's grace?

_____

_____

_____

After a binge and a purge, when shame would slime me with lies of unworthiness, grace was the last thing I thought I deserved or wanted to run to. But it was the one thing I needed more than anything else. Grace gives us the ability, in the midst of our sins, to *run to love as fast as we can*—not so we can keep having the same destructive behaviors, but so that love can heal us.

"What shall we say then? Are we to continue in sin that grace may abound? By no means! How can we who died to sin still live in it? Do you not know that all of us who have been baptized into Christ Jesus were baptized into his death? We were buried therefore with him by baptism into death, so that as Christ was raised from the dead by the glory of the Father, we too might walk in newness of life.

For if we have been united with him in a death like his, we shall certainly be united with him in a resurrection like his. We know that our old self was crucified with him so that the sinful body might be destroyed, and we might no longer be enslaved to sin. For he who has died is freed from sin. But if we have died with Christ, we believe that we shall also live with him. For we know that Christ being raised from the dead will never die again; death no longer has dominion over him. The death he died he died to sin, once for all, but the life he lives he lives to God. So you also must consider yourselves dead to sin and alive to God in Christ Jesus.

Let not sin therefore reign in your mortal bodies, to make you obey their passions. Do not yield your members to sin as instruments of wickedness, but yield yourselves to God as men who have been brought from death to life, and your members to God as instruments of righteousness. For sin will have no dominion over you, since you are not under law but under grace." Romans 6:1-14

Friends, I have good news. If you're in Christ, *you don't have an old, sinful nature anymore.*

That's right, I said it. Scripture said your sin nature has been crucified and destroyed so that you don't have to be a slave to sin anymore. Stop trying to disciple it! Stop trying to resurrect it and make it better! You have to consider yourself dead to sin and alive to Christ—*even while you're still sinning.*

I had years of addictions that didn't just go away after I got saved. The pain in my heart, my thinking, and my beliefs kept the cycle of bad behaviors rolling. The second I would fall; I'd start flogging myself out of anger. The moment I would fail, my entire day was shot. I had no concept of grace as a doorway, bidding me enter into freedom. I wanted to be perfect before feeling worthy to come to God. I wanted to clean myself off before receiving His love.

But that's not the way it works.

Have you struggled with having grace for yourself while you're still struggling? Do you want to be perfect, spotless, and sinless because of your efforts before receiving God's love? Write any hang-ups with grace that you have below.

_____

_____

_____

_____

> *"For by grace you have been saved through faith; and this is not your own doing, it is the gift of God— not because of works, lest any man should boast." Ephesians 2:8-9* (ESV)

If you could earn your way into God's arms of love, then Christ wouldn't have had to die. If you could be spotless enough to be worthy of God's affection, there would be no need for the cross. When you come to God in your struggle, *as you are*, the doorway that grace provides takes you straight to the Healer.

And as the Healer heals, you change. And He gets the glory.

Imagine an action or behavior that you're ashamed of. Now, right after you do the thing you hate, when you feel like you're dripping with slime and shame, I want you to see yourself inside of Christ as a new creation. That old, sin nature that you have has been *destroyed*. You don't have to be a slave to it anymore. Imagine a huge door with the word 'GRACE' over it and *run through that door as fast as you can into the arms of Love.*

Take ten minutes, going back to the obsessions that have shamed your life, and run through the door of grace with each obsession. Run through GRACE with your addictions, your depression, your past, your abortion. Run through GRACE with your body, your soul, and your spirit. See yourself covered, made

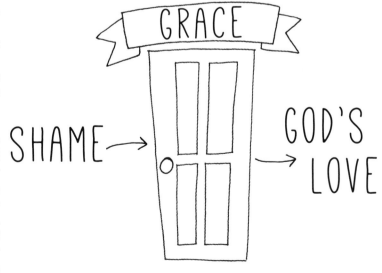

new, and forgiven. Break the shame cycle that keeps you away from the solution.

Run, run, run, run. And never look back.

Write your experience running through GRACE below.

_____

_____

_____

_____

_____

_____

_____

_____

_____

_____

_____

_____

Day 3: **Transference**

Read pages 135-142 in Chapter 7 of God Loves Ugly.

Out of fear of exposure, I covered the pain in my heart through performance as a little girl. If I could just act like everything was sparkly and new, maybe no one would see the disaster going on inside, exposing how shameful and dirty I really was. But the pain was hungry and always demanded more. So then the pain demanded food, then drugs, alcohol and cigarettes, then boys—trying to numb, trying to hide. But the pain was still starving, and my actions were killing me. Then I met Jesus, and I was instantly saved, but my pain didn't instantly go away. I put away the drugs, alcohol and cigarettes as a good Christian girl, but the pain needed to be silenced every day.

When food began killing me and I found myself in rehab, I finally had a controlled environment where my life was not my own. But the pain still demanded to be numbed every day, bringing me full circle back to my first numbing agent in life—performance.

Have you had behaviors that modified over the years, but never truly healed? Write any addictions or behaviors that might have transferred in your life.

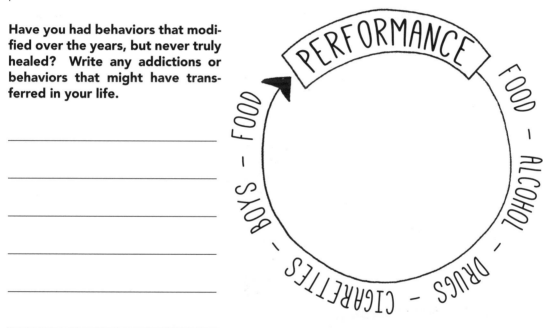

_____

_____

_____

_____

_____

_____

It's very interesting watching shows that help people lose weight, because the weight is only the symptom to the problem. The problem is a heart in pain that craves to be numbed. I've known many people who worked overtime to lose weight, only to find that the weight came back because the problem was never taken care of. I've also known people who succeeded in reaching their goal of weight loss, only to transfer their addiction of overeating onto an obsession with diet and exercise. Unless someone looks anorexic, we don't look at thin people and immediately think 'problem' like we do with someone who's overweight. But a thin person obsessed and in bondage to calories, food, restricting and exercise has just as much of a problem as someone who wears their pain externally in the form of weight.

Maybe you've never struggled with food, and for that, I'm so thankful. An alcoholic doesn't have to walk into a bar, but when you're addicted to food or obsessed with your body, you have to face your problem three times a day in order to live. Maybe you've never been faced with a struggle that's controlled you. But if you ever look in the mirror and struggle with hatred for what you see, then dear friend, you are in pain. And that pain has been numbed *somehow and in some way.*

Have you tried to fix your pain for years—going after the symptom (behaviors) and not the solution (the heart)?   Because of this tactic, have they continued to transfer?

_____

_____

_____

I believed that if I could just be thin and stop bingeing, all my problems would go away. I believed that if I could control myself around food, I would be 'fixed.'

Do you believe, like I did, that being perfect around your struggle would fix the problem?

_____

_____

_____

For years, I had a terrible temper that came out of deep pain. I believed that if I could just manage my anger, the anger would go away. But let me tell you something, trying to bottle up explosive anger only does one thing—causes explosions. Until I stopped trying to manage my anger and asked Jesus to heal the reasons why I was angry in the first place, I stayed furious inside.

Whatever it is that you've tried to fix on your own, when you get it 'under control,' I promise you—something else will always pop up from the pain.

Do you struggle with anger like I did? Are you angry with God? Are you angry with yourself? Does that anger seep out onto the people you love?

_____

_____

_____

It's time to stop the transferring cycle once and for all. And you can't do it alone. Letting someone into your pain breaks the shame cycle, and when shame is broken, you begin to move forward into freedom.

If we could simply go to God and be healed of everything, then He wouldn't have created the church. But the church was His idea, and you need the people just as much as they need you.

> *Therefore, confess your sins to one another and pray for one another, that you may be healed. The prayer of a righteous person has great power as it is working. Hebrews 5:16* (ESV)

Isn't it strange that God wants us to confess sin to one another when He has already forgiven us of all our sins? He knows there's something powerful when you involve someone else into your healing process. Shame is broken, you pray for each other, and you hold each other up. And if you want to be healed, in the fullness of the word, you have to let someone into your mess and walk out life together.

Have you tried to take your struggles to God and change without letting anyone else know? Are you too ashamed of your eating disorder, pornography addiction, depression, sexual issues, fear, etc, so you've kept it a secret—even from those closest to you?

_____

_____

_____

Have you been able to handle your pain on your own with God, or perhaps it might be time to let someone in on your hurt?

_____

_____

_____

_____

This is your week to fully expose yourself to the vulnerability of love. If you've held onto a hidden secret that's been plaguing your life, find someone safe this week and let them in on your shame. It could be a pastor, a therapist, a friend, or a spouse. It could be a coworker or a parent. Whoever it is, it's time to expose yourself before love, confessing this thing that has held you in chains.

Take a moment and write out some options of whom you might be able to expose your pain to.

_____

_____

_____

Do you want to be healed and whole? Then you need people praying for you. Do you want to be free from the transference of pain? Then you need people loving you when you think you're unlovable—no matter what you've done or how bad you think it is. Not everyone is safe, which is why you must be selective in choosing who you let in on your pain. And not all advice is from the Father, so make sure you include someone who believes in the God who heals all hurts. But I promise you—when you're seen as you are and still loved, healing always blooms.

Jesus, give courage where courage is needed. Light a path to freedom, involving the safety of someone on this earth who can love them, even while exposed. Thank you that there's nothing that we've done that cannot be forgiven, and we long for the fullness of that forgiveness. Amen.

Day 4: Family & Forgiveness

Read pages 142-149 and the 'Your Turn' questions on pages 154-156.

I have an incredible family, and unfortunately, that's sometimes rare in this world. The more I hear people's stories, the more I realize that almost every pain in the heart of mankind stems back to the family in some capacity—even with wonderful families like mine.

While in treatment for an eating disorder, my parents were ready to do anything and everything they needed to help their little girl get well, even if that meant admitting they had contributed to the problem. But that wasn't the case for many of my fellow patients. Some of their parents wouldn't dare show up out of embarrassment and were so ashamed that they avoided the situation and their children altogether.

Take a minute and describe your family. Be brutally honest—no one is going to read this but you.

Do you feel like you were loved and wanted growing up? Were your parents verbally abusive, or maybe physically or sexually? Did you not have a family at all and grew up in the foster system? Were your parents divorced and you got stuck in the crossfire? Take a few minutes and write out a thorough description of your family dynamics—the good, the bad, and the honest.

_____

_____

_____

_____

_____

As a parent myself, I'm extremely aware of how my words and actions will either hinder or help shape my child. The way I speak to my husband, the way I allow my heart to heal, the tone of my voice, the way I deal with stressful situations—my son Moses takes it in like a sponge and it defines his little world.

Dysfunction passes down from mothers and fathers to daughters and sons whether we want it to or not. Which is why it's so important for you to be healed so you stop the cycle continuing in your family line. (And even if you're later in years and felt guilty as you read that sentence, don't you dare! God loves taking broken situations and redeeming them!)

Are there things about you that you know stemmed from your family? Are you exactly like your mother or your father? Did you pick up characteristics that you

hate or that you love? Take a moment and write out character and personality traits that came from your family line that you wish you could change.

_____

_____

_____

Wounds from a family member can be the hardest wounds to let go of—especially if it was a parent you expected to love and protect you. Attachment pain is the deepest pain the heart can face, and it begins in the home as a baby. If you feel let down by a parent, grandparent, aunt or uncle and have held onto offense, bitterness, unforgiveness, and accusation, you're probably exhausted. I know I was.

My entire life, I'd built a case against my mother. I judged and hated things about her. I hurled my onslaught of stones and as a result, we definitely had our fair share of verbal throw downs. I thought that as the parent, she should be the one to always fix things, and I took little responsibility for my part in the cycle.

One day back in my twenties, after one of our usual knock down-drag out yelling matches, I heard the Holy Spirit whisper to my heart, _'Love covers a multitude of sins.'_ I didn't want to love her. I wanted her to love me first and be the parent! But the older I got, the more I realized...

I have to take ownership of my actions, regardless of what our history has been.

Do you want a parent to prove that they love you first by taking the first step to do the right thing? Do you think it's possible to cover a multitude of their sins with forgiveness, choosing to love them regardless of your history?

_____

_____

_____

By the way, forgiveness doesn't necessarily mean reconciliation for the relationship. If you've been the victim of abuse, or a relationship that consistently destroyed your life, boundaries aren't 'unchristian.' They're the right thing to do.   You can forgive someone but still draw a boundary for a destructive relationship.

And if you answered 'no' to the question above, feeling like it might kill you to take the high road and love them despite all they've done to hurt you, then all is not lost. In order to forgive, you must know that you're forgiven.

The greatest mystery of salvation is how God forgives every one of our sins _even before we commit them._ The sin that you might commit tomorrow has already been forgiven. The sins that you'll commit in twenty years, they're forgiven, too. The mercy of God to forgive is astounding and goes far beyond reason or logic. Which is why, once again, it isn't something that can be earned.

It's a gift that must be received through Christ.

I just read an article of a mother embracing her daughter's killer in court. He had brought a gun on the bus and after deciding to show it off, a bullet accidentally shot her daughter in the neck. She made a plea to the court not to send this boy to jail, but to help him rehabilitate himself by giving speeches on the dangers of guns in school. And as he left in chains, she threw her arms around the boy who had taken her daughter away from her.

That boy didn't deserve forgiveness. And neither do you.

But we get the gift anyway.

Do you feel unworthy to receive forgiveness for all that you've done? When you look at God's unlimited supply of forgiveness for you, are you ashamed to fully receive it?

_____

_____

_____

Write out all the things about your life that you believe are hard to forgive in the bucket to the right. After you've written them inside, take a moment and receive His gift of forgiveness again, looking at the forgiveness that is more powerful than your sin.

Drink it in.

Let it soak into the cracks of your heart.

Let it overtake you.

Is it hard to believe God can forgive all the things you haven't forgiven yourself for?

_____

_____

_____

The hardest part about forgiveness isn't letting others off the hook—it's letting ourselves off the hook. We know what we're really like. We know what we deserve, and we usually like enforcing our self-imposed sentence. When it comes to getting free, our worst enemy isn't always the people who have wronged us—it's the jailer who holds the keys to our freedom.

And dear friend, you're the one who holds the keys.

Take a moment and look at the FORGIVEN bucket on the previous page, filled with all the things you have a hard time forgiving about yourself. Go stand in front of a mirror, look deep into your eyes, take the keys to your freedom and *let yourself go.*

Forgive yourself, even if you don't think you deserve it. Forgive yourself, even if you were the one who was wrong. When you start to doubt, take a step back and receive the gift of God's forgiveness again, stepping forward to forgive yourself yet again. Give yourself the gift that God has given you.

Go to a mirror NOW (even if it means running to the loo!) and begin to forgive yourself.

How did this make you feel? Was it hard? Was it liberating? If you did this on a regular basis, what do you think would happen? Write your answers below.

_____

_____

_____

_____

_____

Now that you've begun to receive God's gift of forgiveness, and you've given yourself the gift of forgiveness, it's time to give that gift away.

Who do you need to forgive?

Was it a parent, teacher, friend, all of the above? Was it a bully, a spouse, a child?

Who has wounded you so badly, that wound has gone unhealed? It's time for you to *heal*.

Take as much time as you need to make this list. Go back as far as you need— even if it's early on in childhood. You don't have to recount all that was done, but I guarantee you, your heart hasn't forgotten who did it. If you need to forgive someone, write their name in the space below.

_____

_____

_____

_____

You might not feel like forgiving, and that's okay. Forgiveness is a choice, and not always a feeling. But I find the feeling can come if I take a minute and ask God for **grace.**

For each person on your list, take a moment and ask God what *He sees about the person*. Ask Him to see the reasons behind their behaviors, their accusations, their cruelty. Ask Father if you can see them through the doorway of grace—just like He sees you.

And as you see them, compassion just might fill your heart. And as you look for their true nature, and not just what they've done to you, you might actually feel sympathy for them. As you begin to see, let your heart begin to forgive.

Go down the list, taking as much time as you need, wiping the slate clean in your heart, learning to truly forgive.

Day 5: **Freedom**

Read 'Freedom,' pages 149-153.

You will always be this way. You will always struggle with this. You will always be just like your mother. You will always be fat. You will always be poor. You will always be ugly. You're too screwed up to ever be happy. You will always hurt. You will always be a mess.

You will never be free.

If we're honest, we've probably all had a few of these thoughts, if not all of them. There's always something that seems bigger than our ability to overcome it, and before long, our thoughts have come into agreement with the problem—instead of the solution.

While in therapy, my very well meaning Christian counselor told me I would learn the tools to be able to manage my addiction, but that I was going to struggle with food for the rest of my life.

Is there a personality trait, struggle, addiction, or state of mind that you've felt this way about? Have you tried over and over to change with little to no results, so you think this is just the way life has to be? Are you managing pain because you don't know how to get rid of it? Write out any things about yourself or your life that you'd like to change, but deep down, you believe they'll never fully change.

_____

_____

_____

_____

Has God been powerful in your life, or are you uncertain if He can truly transform your heart and life? If you've seen or experienced a powerless God, describe how it's influenced your perception of Him. Or, have you seen God move in your life? Write out and remember all the times He's clearly intervened in your life.

_____

_____

_____

_____

On page 151, I finally put my foot down, making a declaration that addictions and dysfunction would no longer transfer in my life. I was ready to surrender to a God who had to heal the leaky bucket of my wounded heart. **If you've already put your foot down or are ready to do this, write out a declaration in the space below**.

_____

_____

_____

_____

You've uncovered the lies you believe from your negative experiences and now realize you can challenge those beliefs. **Have you been doing this?**   ☐ YES   ☐ NO

You've uncovered the word curses that contributed to the problem and know how to challenge those lying words with the truth. **Have you been doing this?**   ☐ YES   ☐ NO

You've been taking stock of your emotions, knowing they come from your thoughts, beliefs, and can _choose_ to have power over them. **Have you been doing this?**   ☐ YES   ☐ NO

You've realized your actions come from your beliefs, so instead of trying to change your negative actions, you can take the pain in your heart directly to the Healer. **Have you been doing this?**   ☐ YES   ☐ NO

You've encountered a powerful God whose design and plan was to love you into wholeness, and because the veil is torn, His presence lives inside of you, and the Counselor Holy Spirit leads you into all truth, you can experience His love. **Have you been doing this?**   ☐ YES   ☐ NO

You've realized holding onto bitterness, unforgiveness, and offense is a load you can't carry if you're ever going to be free, and learned how to surrender your pain. **Have you done this?**   ☐ YES   ☐ NO

You've seen the shame—fear—control cycle and know that introducing shame to Love produces good fruit. **Have you been doing this?**   ☐ YES   ☐ NO

Checking 'yes' to each box is putting your foot down, and is the ultimate goal. We all want our Promised Land of freedom, but we're going to have to kick off the giants before we can inhabit the land. And once you get the giants off, _you have to defend your land to keep them from coming back._

If you checked 'no' to any of the boxes, then you still have giants in your land, and it's time to get serious about inhabiting freedom. If you partner with the Healer, taking your free will and submitting it to His truth, His presence, and His healing—the power of God goes before you to drive the enemy back.

It's time to possess your land of freedom.

If you're anything like me, you wanted to snap your fingers and never struggle again. I have news for you, that's probably not going to happen. Walking into my Promised Land built spiritual, emotional, and physical muscles. Walking into my freedom with God built a history with Him that I couldn't have had otherwise. I learned to trust Him. I learned that He loved me even when I fell. I learned to have grace for myself— because He has grace for me.

If you're struggling with something right now that's consuming your life, take a moment and write out a prayer of grace for yourself below. Let yourself off the 'perfect hook.' Give yourself grace to walk this journey of surrender, history, romance, and freedom with the Healer. And every time you fall, He's right there to pick you back up—unashamed of you.

I, _____, give myself grace for the journey of inhabiting my Promised Land. If I fall, I'll let Love pick me up. If I stumble, I won't partner with shame, I'll cover myself in the grace I've been given that empowers me to freedom, running back into the arms of my God. (Write anything else you'd like to add below.)

_____

_____

_____

_____

Love breaks your chains, dear one. Not perfect behavior. Love sets you free, not striving. I'm completely free from my eating disorder because I didn't go after the food. I went after the pain, introducing it to Love every time I fell, and one day the pain was so healed, I didn't need the food to medicate anymore.

Does focusing on being loved instead of trying to fix your 'problem' make sense? Has it already started to work?

_____

_____

_____

Take a moment and note any changes since you began this study. Are you experiencing freedom? Are you experiencing God? Are you finding it easier to catch old emotions or actions before they turn into cycles of destruction? Write your progress, successes, and triumphs below.

_____

_____

_____

_____

_____

_____

_____

_____

_____

_____

_____

_____

_____

_____

_____

_____

_____

_____

Week 7: GROUP DISCUSSION QUESTIONS

Chapter 6, *Monsters* & Chapter 7, *Forty Days and a Horse*

1 **Begin with a prayer, thanking God that His Spirit will lead you into all truth. (John 16:13-15)**

2 **Read the 'We Believe God Can' list aloud.** Set your faith on the promise that God has already overcome your current struggle. Briefly give any testimony of your declarations blooming to life over the past week.

3 **Discussion Questions:**

• Tell the group one new belief that you're beginning to live out every day!

• Chapter 6 went into detail about my main struggle, which was food. You may have never battled addiction, but you might have something that steals from your joy. If you feel safe to share, what are some of the hidden monsters that have devoured your life over the years?

• Have you tried to keep these behaviors hidden from God and the people around you? Has this approach helped or hurt you?

• What negative thoughts have turned into harmful actions or obsessions? Do you see how changing your thinking might change your behaviors?

• Is there something that you just can't get free from on your own? (Do not share if you don't feel safe, but if you do, now is the time to break the shame cycle and ask for help).

• In Chapter 7, you learned about the transference of coping mechanisms. Were you able to trace back any means of coping in your own life?

• Performance and perfectionism are common in our culture, attempting to hide the past to avoid rejection. Has performance played a role in your life? Are you afraid if people truly see you, they will reject you?

• Everyone has family issues. Is there someone in your family who triggers you the most? If so, have you forgiven them? (Remember, forgiveness isn't a feeling, it's a choice).

• If you find it hard to forgive others, you might be rejecting or trying to earn forgiveness from the Father. Why is it important to receive God's forgiveness in order for you to forgive yourself and others?

4 **Close with a prayer, thanking God for all He's done and all that He's going to do.**

5 **Have *Chapter 8* and the assignments completed by the next time you meet. (Pages 158-180)**

week eight
Chapter 8 Lessons in Love

Day 1: **Rearview Mirror**

Read pages 161-166 in *God Loves Ugly*.

Before we get started today, let me say one thing.

You are not strange for wanting relationship. You are not weird for wanting someone to be attracted to you, or to choose you over everyone else in the world. You're not insecure for longing to be beautiful, adored, and cherished. It's in your DNA, because you're created in the image of a God who longs for relationship.

There's a reason why God looked at Adam in Genesis 2:18 and said "It's not good for man to be alone. I will make a helper suitable for him." You were made to be loved, and God uses earthly relationships to shower love on us from all sides. Jesus continues to love and heal me *through* the arms of my Studhubs every single day. God's first blessing proclaimed to mankind wouldn't have been to 'be fruitful and multiply' in Genesis 1:28 if He didn't want us to have earthly relationships—mirroring and reflecting the intimacy we have with Him.

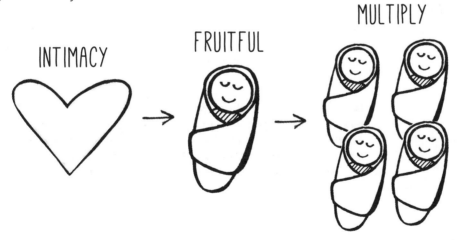

Take a deep sigh and write out the words below: "I was made for relationship. I was made to want to be wanted. This does not make me weak. This does not make me insecure. This makes me normal, created in the image of a God who also wants to be wanted."

_____

_____

_____

Now, here's the catch. Longing for relationship can't come from a place of lack—otherwise it always produces insecurity if someone doesn't want us back. Longing for relationship has to come from a place of identity. It has to come from a foundational knowing that we were created for relationship, so we long for it because it's in our DNA.

Take a moment and think about your desire for romantic relationship. You might have already been in a marriage for decades. You might be single with no prospects on the horizon. You might be a dater who's afraid of commitment. You might be a teenager falling in and out of crushes. Wherever you are on this journey of intimate love, write about your longing, or lack of longing, for romantic intimacy.

_____

_____

_____

Intimacy means "In—To—Me—See." See everything, and love me anyway.

In Genesis 2 when Adam and Eve were formed in the garden, they were completely naked in front of one another, and in front of God. They were completely seen and loved as they were, without shame.

You were created for that kind of intimacy, where you're completely seen—the good, the bad, the beautiful, and the ugly—and loved no matter what. That kind of love brings freedom. That kind of love brings life.

Is intimacy a hard thing for you? Are you afraid if anyone ever sees all of you, knowing everything, they will reject you? Maybe this has already been your experience with earthly relationships. Write out any ways that earthly intimacy has hurt you, as opposed to loving you unconditionally.

_____

_____

_____

_____

_____

My deepest desire as a single girl was to be chosen by a guy. The problem was, guys had been the deepest source of my pain—from rejection, to abuse, to bullying, to everything in between. This longing for the love of a man proved that my heart was wired for affection—I wanted something desperately even though it had a history of destroying me.

Do you want romantic love but deep down, your heart believes you don't deserve it? Or maybe you're already in a committed relationship, but there's still something deep inside that doesn't believe you deserve to be cherished and adored? Maybe you don't have any problem being loved. Write out how you truly believe you deserve to be loved in the space below.

_____

_____

_____

You don't necessarily attract what you want. You attract who you are. You attract what you think you're worth.

Our actions always follow our beliefs, and because I believed I was going to be rejected because of past experiences, I acted rejected around guys. Because I acted rejected around guys, I *was* rejected over and over.

Has this been true in your own life? Do you see how you might be attracting, or have attracted, what you believed you deserved, instead of what you truly wanted? Are you behaving according to what you believe? Write out your history of attraction below and look for patterns and themes.

_____

_____

_____

_____

The enemy loves to torment us where we've agreed with his lies. There was something powerful that happened that day in the car when I looked into my rearview mirror, breaking old agreements with rejection. I declared truth that bubbled up from my heart, and that truth broke chains.

Do you need a rearview mirror experience like the one that I had?

"So faith comes from hearing, and hearing through the word of Christ." Romans 10:17 (ESV)

If you need faith to believe, maybe you need to hear truth first. And in order to hear, your heart needs to listen. You can tell yourself that you are worthy of love until you're blue in the face, but you won't believe it until you *hear* it from the One who knows you better than you know yourself.

Take a few minutes, get quiet, and listen to the Holy Spirit. What does He have to say about your worth? Does He believe you're worthy of being loved? Does He love you unconditionally? How does He see you? Close your eyes, still your mind and heart, and listen to His voice. Write out all the amazing things He has to say about you below. (And remember, you're no longer under condemnation, so if you're hearing a condemning tone, it's probably the accuser or your internal critic, and not the Spirit of truth!)

_____

_____

_____

_____

_____

Now that you've heard what Father has to say about you, I want you to come into agreement with it. Get in front of a mirror, look deep into your own eyes, and repeat the things God said about your worth, your beauty, your heart, your healing, and your future.

I AM _____

_____

_____

_____

Thank you, Father, that You are light and in You is no darkness at all. (I John 1:5). Thank you that when You shine Your light on our lives, it's always done in love. Thank you that Your light purifies, redeems, restores, and sets free. Thank you that Your light isn't scary—to be seen by You is to be seen by Love. Thank you that as You see me—all of me—telling me what You see, I can come into agreement with heaven.

And because You love me without shame or blame, I can learn to love myself. Amen.

Day 2: The Chase

Read 'The X-Factor,' and 'The Chase' on pages 167-172.

We all see beauty through a lens, and culture influences our personal lenses more than anything else.

For the Pa Dong tribe along the Thai/Burmese border, elongated necks are a sign of beauty, and brass rings are added to a girl's neck at the age of six to begin the elongation process. For Karo girls in southern Ethiopia, the skin on their stomachs are cut to create scars, and when they have enough scars, they're ready and beautiful enough for marriage. In many African countries such as Nigeria and Mauritania, women are fed as much as possible to make them more beautiful, and thin women are pitied. Years ago in China, tiny feet made a woman desirable, so many parents would allow their daughters feet to be broken and bound tightly to keep the feet small, causing lifelong pain and difficulty walking. Even in our Western culture, one race prefers curves while another celebrates emaciation.

Beauty has so many different definitions throughout the world, and many of those definitions have influenced your vision without you even knowing it.

What is your definition of beauty? What would it take for you to be considered beautiful? Write down any physical, circumstantial, or societal factors that contribute to your personal definition of beauty.

_____

_____

_____

We all see ourselves through our lens of beliefs. Write down several main beliefs you have about true beauty on the mirror below, then draw a picture of how that definition influences your perception. How does that definition cause you to see yourself?

MIRROR, MIRROR

PERCEPTION

For years, I believed that in order to be beautiful, I had to have a teeny, tiny, tight bottom that looked like I did a *Brazilian Butt Lift* DVD on a daily basis. So every time I looked in the mirror, I judged my backside through this distorted definition of beauty. No matter what the reality was, my poor, non-Brazilian backside never measured up.

When you believe you don't measure up, your emotions are bombarded will all sorts of insecurities.

If you haven't achieved your personal definition of beauty written above, do your perceived inadequacies influence your emotions? How do you feel being 'less than' your beauty list?

_____

_____

_____

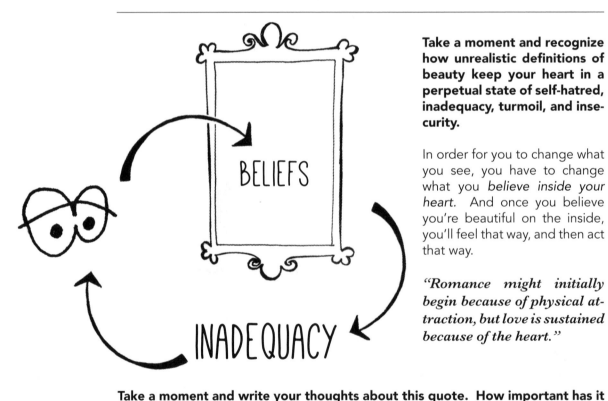

BELIEFS

INADEQUACY

Take a moment and recognize how unrealistic definitions of beauty keep your heart in a perpetual state of self-hatred, inadequacy, turmoil, and insecurity.

In order for you to change what you see, you have to change what you *believe inside your heart.* And once you believe you're beautiful on the inside, you'll feel that way, and then act that way.

"Romance might initially begin because of physical attraction, but love is sustained because of the heart."

Take a moment and write your thoughts about this quote. How important has it been for you to cultivate beauty inside of your heart? Have you focused more on your outward beauty, or your inward beauty?

_____

_____

_____

_____

On page 170 in *God Loves Ugly*, you read about the list of attributes I wanted in a husband. **If you're single, take a moment and write out items you're looking for in a life partner. And if you're already married, write out a thorough description of your spouse below.**

_____

_____

_____

SINGLES: How many characteristics are on your list because of insecurity, like my need for wanting my future husband to be taller than me in heels and older than me? And then, how many characteristics are on your list out of your identity of what you're worth?

SPOUSES: How many characteristics did you list that are seen through past pain and hurt? How many are critical? And now, how many are listed through the eyes of hope, seeing your spouse as God sees them?

_____

_____

_____

How we see ourselves determines how we see others. For many years, I was extremely critical of what I wanted in a man because I was extremely critical of myself. And then when I got that amazing man, I had to learn to remove my critical lens so that it didn't affect how I saw him.

Do you have a critical lens in front of your eyes?
Do you see yourself through the lens of criticism,   ☐ YES ☐ NO
and then see your loved ones through that same lens?

If the answer is yes, take a moment and pray.

Place your hands on your eyes, get quiet, and ask Father to remove any critical lenses that are blurring your vision. Ask Jesus to wipe your vision clean by cleaning out your heart with His truth, His grace, and His kindness. Ask the Holy Spirit to speak to the core of your being, whispering how He sees you and how He wants you to see.

Take several minutes to bask in this newness, let Him give your heart new sight. Write everything you experience, feel, hear, and see below.

_____

_____

_____

Day 3: **The Difference Between Love & Sex**

Read 'Most Precious Possession' on pages 172-176.

If I always did what I felt like doing, I'd be in real trouble. I'd spout out terrible word daggers after strangers cut me off in traffic, and I'd never eat a nutrient. My diet would most likely consist of burgers, pizza, and chocolate. I'd stay in bed every morning far later than a mother of a toddler ever should, and I'd definitely never see the inside of a gym. But as we've learned over the weeks of this study, feelings come from somewhere.

They come from your heart.

> *"The heart is deceitful above all things, and it is exceedingly corrupt: who can know it?" Jeremiah 17:9* (ASV)

Your heart isn't bad—in fact, it's filled with the Spirit of truth if you're in Christ, and your sin nature has been crucified! But even though your heart is filled with the Holy Spirit of the living God, it can still be deceived based upon your beliefs. And when your heart is deceived, you act deceived.

> *"I, the LORD, search the heart, I test the mind, Even to give to each man according to his ways, according to the results of his deeds." Jeremiah 17:20 (NASB)*

This verse brings me so much comfort. For years while struggling with an eating disorder, God didn't look at my deeds like I did—He tested my heart, knowing my actions originated there. He saw how much I hated my destructive behaviors, trapped in cycles of addiction that I didn't know how to get free from. For years while running to random guys, making out at parties with anyone who would have me, God didn't just look at the negative actions and ways. He looked at my broken heart—the deceived heart longing to be loved, trying to fill that longing with the counterfeit affection of a man.

God sees the full picture—not just the action.

Since beginning this study, have you begun to focus more on your heart, and not just your actions? How has this affected your life?

_____

_____

_____

Your heart is everything, dear friend. It's your control center, your decision maker, and whatever is allowed to remain inside determines the outcome of your life. There's a reason God tells us in Proverbs 4:23:

"Guard your heart above all else,
for it determines the course of your life." (NLT)

When looking for romantic love, have you viewed your heart as your most precious possession, both to guard, and then to give as a gift? Or have you not given much thought about the worth of your heart—and someone else's heart—within a relationship?

_____

_____

_____

In our sex-saturated culture, the lines between love and sex can become very blurry. In fact, most examples on television and in movies display the cart far out in front of the horse—urging people to jump into bed with someone to see if love can be cultivated.

"Inside the parameters of love, sex is unsurpassable. It brings two people closer together than they ever could have imagined. But it doesn't create love. It enhances it." -page 173, *God Loves Ugly*

God created sex, which means, sex isn't bad. It's really, really good, because He doesn't create anything that isn't good. The reason why God put a covenant of marriage around sexual intimacy isn't because He's a mean Father who wants to keep us all from having fun. It's because He wants to protect us out of love.

When you get married, ugly character traits, behaviors, and heart issues are going to arise simply because we're all in a process of *becoming*. And when those ugly, nasty, not so beautiful things begin to surface, the covenant of marriage protects us as we help to love each other into wholeness. If my love for Studhubs was contingent on him being perfect, and if his love was contingent on me being perfect, we'd both be in trouble. But as the ugly parts have surfaced over the last seven years, we've made a covenant before God, friends, and family to stick it out—even as the storms come.

We've chosen to be *one flesh* as we become all God wants us to be. Which means, we're in this thing together, even when the refinement fire gets really, really hot.

What are some ways a covenant of marriage could protect your heart, instead of tie you down or lock you in? Have you ever thought of covenant as protection before?

_____

_____

_____

Sex inside of covenant is the safest place I've ever known. Studhubs and I have committed to be naked in every other area of our lives—emotionally, spiritually—so physical nakedness becomes so natural inside the safety of covenant. And once we're exposed in every area, committing to love one another, sex and oneness can become a place of deep healing.

Here's the icing on the cake—that intimacy creates *life*.

Where did you get your definition of sex? Did it come from movies, television shows, books, or church? Have you viewed sex as being 'bad' because you grew up in a religious culture where it was seen as wrong, or was sex something that was normal outside of marriage? Write your paradigm of sex below and where it came from.

_____

_____

_____

Have you confused love and sex in the past? Have you given sex in hopes of obtaining love? Write your answers below.

_____

_____

_____

If sex outside of covenant has been a normal part of your life and past, write out ways that it created permanent healing, and write out ways that it produced pain:

LIFE   PAIN

_____   _____

_____   _____

_____   _____

_____   _____

_____   _____

Sex outside of covenant is dangerous simply because of this: you become 'one flesh' with someone who has no responsibility to love you. And at the end of the day, your heart was made to be loved.

Good news—there's redemption for *everything*. If you've looked for love through sex in the past and come up empty, or ended up with a tattered heart that feels lonelier than ever, God can heal the brokenness of your past, healing the root issue, and *you can live free from that pain.*

<hr />

1. If you've been 'one flesh' with anyone in the past outside of covenant—even if you're now married and it's been long ago—take a moment and pray this prayer if you haven't prayed something like it before:

Father, I want true intimacy. I want intimacy that sees all of me and loves me anyway, and I want to be completely free from the sexual brokenness of my past. Every person I've become 'one' with outside of covenant, I break every place where my soul was bound with theirs. I break every place where my soul was tied with _____(get specific here and say names), and I come into agreement with Your truth—that I'm pure because I'm in Christ! Thank you, God, that You are filling every place in my heart that needs healing. You are filling me with overflowing. I say NO to the enemy and his legal ground to keep me tied up from the sexual sins of my past. I say YES to the redemption of Jesus who broke every curse.

Thank you, Jesus, amen!

2. If you're single and waiting for your someday spouse, make a commitment right now to separate sex and love, guarding your heart for true intimacy until you're bound within covenant:

I, _____, commit to guarding my heart above all else, knowing the condition of my heart determines the course of my life. I commit to true intimacy above all else, knowing that my heart wants and needs love more than anything else. I commit to submitting my heart to the Healer, becoming all I am created to be. I commit to becoming someone so filled with Love, I have so much love to give away. And I commit to guard my body for true intimacy and oneness inside the covenant of marriage. Amen.

3. If you're already married and in a covenant, take a moment to commit, once again, to sexual intimacy within your marriage. God created sex to bring two people together with pleasure—it's a part of the process. If you have a healthy sex life within your marriage, then take a moment and thank God for it. And if sexual intimacy is something that's been a mystery, talk to God about it. Tell Him how you don't understand it. Ask Him to show you the fullness of what He created it to be—to bring intimacy, pleasure, oneness and *life.*

Day 4: **Wholeness**

Read 'Wholeness' on pages 176-178.

My good friend Tyler Ward, author of the incredible marriage book *Marriage Rebranded*, compiled a free eBook called *Marriage Hacks: 25 Practical Ways To Make Love Last*. Within this eBook, 25 different Christian leaders—from Gary Chapman, W.P. Young, and Danny Silk—give relational advice for married couples and singles that are looking to be married someday.

I wrote briefly about Studhub's process of helping me walk into freedom from my eating disorder in *God Loves Ugly*, but you deserve the whole story. It's just that good of a story. And since I wrote out the full story in *Marriage Hacks*, I thought I'd share it with you below, hopefully enticing you to download the entire eBook.

LEARNING TO BE NAKED WITHOUT FEAR

"As my husband Lucas turned up the volume on our television that particular day in August 2007, his efforts to drown out the lawn mower next door did little to drown out the worried thoughts screaming inside my head.

For years, I'd been a touring musician, traveling the world and playing with all sorts of artists—the most recent being Christian music legend Michael W. Smith. In an attempt to be a newlywed who wasn't leaving on a tour bus every few days, we made the decision that I'd quit traveling to enjoy this new marriage situation. But with neither of us bringing in steady income, our choice also left us enjoying an old upstairs apartment with low ceilings, a collection of donated furniture, bright pink carpet that reeked of cigarette smoke, stacks of unpaid bills, and a kitchen stocked with packets of Ramen Noodles.

That day in August as I cuddled up to my fabulous—but very broke—new husband on our second-hand couch, the strength of his arms around me wasn't making the anxiety of our present financial situation go away. Before I was even conscious of the downward spiral, questions about our unknown future had poisoned my heart like a plague. I found myself drowning inside very real, very crippling fear.

What if we can't pay rent this month? What if our only car goes on the brink? What if our cell phones get shut off? What if I don't start touring again? Will we be able to eat this month?

"Babe," I said with an attempted smile, "I'm just going to run to the bathroom for a minute." I lifted his arm off of my shoulder and acted like I was headed back to the loo, then made a quick detour into our little kitchen. I've had years of practice at sneaking food to medicate the pain inside my heart. So it was with great expertise I quietly opened the fridge and began my usual routine, devouring anything and everything I could find.

We didn't have much in stock, but whatever we had, I was going to destroy as fast as I could. Then I would return to his unsuspecting arms, acting as if nothing had ever happened.

When Lucas married me, he knew I had struggled with an eating disorder in the past. He knew I'd been admitted to inpatient treatment with years of counseling under my belt. He even knew that, when the pain of life became uncontrollable, sometimes food was the one thing I still attempted to control. Every once in a blue moon, I'd finally let him in and confess a bingeing episode, long after the binge was over with. But most times, I was far too embarrassed about my food addiction to fully disclose all the ugly details.

So there I was, shoving an oversized bite of leftovers into my mouth—noodles still hanging out and dripping down my chin—when I froze suddenly. Someone was behind me. Someone was watching me. Someone was seeing my shame—was seeing the one thing that made me completely unlovable, or so I believed. I turned around slowly, dreading the look of disgust I was sure to see, the judgment, the fury of hatred—the same hatred I had for myself.

But far from condemnation, this new husband of mine had something on his face I never expected to see. He was grinning ear to ear.

Pulling himself up backwards onto the counter and popping open a bag of chips, he looked into my eyes with the same love I'd seen on the day we made our vows to one another. He looked at this bingeing wife with the same affection he had when he looked at his spotless bride dressed in white.

"Baby," he said quietly. "If you need to binge, I'm going to binge with you. I don't want you do it alone anymore."

Something powerful happened to us in that moment: two became one.

Marriage gives two people the difficult but incredible opportunity to be completely naked in front of each other—physically, emotionally, and spiritually. The problem is, most of us have parts of our lives we're terrified of anyone seeing. But if full exposure isn't allowed, if we're not able to reveal everything about ourselves (good, bad and ugly) within the covenant of marriage, true intimacy can never happen.

Intimacy means "in-to-me-see"—see everything, and love me anyway.

When I first got married to my husband, I truly believed certain parts of my life made me unlovable. I believed that if he saw everything, he would hate me as much as I hated myself. But marriage isn't about perfect people finding a perfect mate. It's about two imperfect souls coming together as one, making a covenant to stick around when the ugly parts get exposed, and then loving each other with grace and understanding while helping each other walk into wholeness.

Just like Lucas did that day when he caught me bingeing.

You see, something healed inside my heart in August 2007 when I was forced to be naked in front of my husband, exposing the shame of my addiction. Instead of being rejected, as I had feared—instead of being yelled at, judged or condemned—he had done the exact opposite. He looked at me inside of my dirty pigpen, sat down, kissed my shameful wounds, and committed to walk beside me—no matter the outcome.

His love that day wasn't laced with an agenda for me to change—but the amazing thing about love is, it ends up changing everything anyway.

In the days and months that followed, our financial situation didn't improve much. But when the anxiety began to rise up like a monster, I had a new place to run—I could run into the arms of love. When insecurities and fears would surface and expose even more ugly behaviors, I knew I had a man who had made a covenant to love me—all of me—no matter how messy it got.

Within that covenant, I was finally safe to let my walls down and be seen.

As he saw, he loved.
As he loved, I changed.
As I changed, we were both set free.

For the rest of our lives, Lucas and I have the great privilege of subjecting ourselves to vulnerability—even as all sorts of behaviors, fears, and insecurities are revealed. We've put all our secrets on the table, knowing that intimacy can only happen when everything is in the light. We've wrapped ourselves in the unending circle of a covenant, committing to love the good along with the bad.

And now, the nakedness I once feared continues to expose my heart to the safe harbor of healing love."

Most times, we want to change in order to be lovable. But what if being loved as we are is what ends up changing everything?

Have you believed that in order to be loved, you have to change? Write your thoughts below.

_____

_____

_____

The beautiful thing about my Studhubs is he was Jesus with flesh on. He mirrored what Father does in our lives every, single day. God sees us—all of us—and loves us anyway.

"For God so loved the world, that he gave his only Son, that whoever believes in him should not perish but have eternal life." John 3:16 (ESV)

God's love for you preceded your birth. God's love was in existence before you ever sinned. God's love for you was tangible before the foundations of the earth. In fact, God gives Love so that everything about your past, present, and future can change.

Have you ever thought about how God's love for you began before you ever took a breath? Write out your thoughts below.

_____

_____

_____

Not every spouse in the world has the capacity to do what my husband did—because not every person in the world understands and has experienced this kind of grace and unconditional love.

Maybe you're married, and this description is far from your significant other. Maybe you've dated in the past, and you've been rejected because of your pain. Maybe your experience with love on this earth has been the exact opposite of the experience I described above.

God is waiting to love you into wholeness. That love WILL change you, and as a result, you'll have an abundance of love to give away.

If you're married, stop waiting for your spouse to love you unconditionally. Let Father love you, heal you, and then you can begin to love your spouse unconditionally. Inside of your marriage, begin to give whatever you would like to receive.

If you're single, focus on receiving from Father every single day—healing your heart, restoring your heart, reviving your soul. Let the true Healer begin to love you into wholeness.

Take ten minutes today and invite Love into the parts of your life that you believe are completely unlovable. Take off the fig leaves once again, and leave yourself exposed before Father. He sees everything and loves you anyway—you might as well stop trying to hide or change yourself.

After you've gotten quiet and let the liquid gold of His love go deep into every crack, begin strategizing with heaven so you can begin overflowing love to those you're in relationship with. Begin to scheme with Jesus how you can love your spouse unconditionally. Begin to partner with the Holy Spirit—dreaming, praying, and asking for your future spouse.

Write your experience, your prayers, and His answers below.

_____

_____

_____

_____

_____

_____

_____

_____

_____

_____

_____

_____

_____

_____

_____

_____

_____

_____

_____

_____

_____

_____

You can download *Marriage Hacks: 25 Practical Ways To Make Love Last* for free at http://www.tylerwardis.com/marriagehacks/

Day 5: **The Love Letter**

Read 'Your Turn' on pages 179-180.

You receive love.

Love changes you.

You overflow love.

The most important part about your life doesn't involve what you give. The most important part of your life involves what you receive *so that you have something to give.*

> *"Cease striving and know that I am God;" Psalm 46:10* (NASB)

Take ten minutes and quiet your heart before Love. Stop your striving, your worship, and your doing—and just *be*. *Position your heart to receive.* Sit in the reality that you've never been separated from the love of God. Bask in the truth that you're lovable as you are—even while you're changing. Meditate on the truth that you're no longer under condemnation—you're the righteousness of God in Christ! Still your heart to listen to His truth. Listen until you hear how much He adores you.

Write down what you hear. Write down all the amazing things God thinks about you. His thoughts outnumber the grains of the sand, and those thoughts are rooted and grounded in love. Write down the details He loves about your personality, your quirks, your smile. Listen to how heaven sees you, and write everything down. (No negatives, please! This is a good indicator that you might be listening to another source—the hurt in your heart or the accuser! God always calls you upwards into all that's available to you in Christ!)

_____

_____

_____

_____

_____

_____

Now that you've heard how heaven sees you, take that perspective and write out a love letter to yourself—seeing from heaven to earth.

Read the 'love letter' portion of the 'Your Turn' section on page 180 in _God Loves Ugly_ and follow the directions. Begin compiling a beautiful love letter to yourself below.

_____

_____

_____

_____

_____

_____

_____

_____

_____

_____

Now, take your newly crafted letter, go in front of the mirror and begin to read. Pause to look deep into your own eyes. Repeat sentences that sting a bit, but that your weary heart might need to hear again. Listen to yourself, bless yourself, and speak words of life over yourself.

The results might surprise you.

Week 8: **GROUP DISCUSSION QUESTIONS**

Chapter 8, _Lessons in Love_

1 **Begin with a prayer, thanking God that all things are possible for those who believe! (Mark 9:23)**

2 **Read the 'We Believe God Can' list aloud.** Partner your faith with His promises once again, declaring that you believe Him! Briefly give any testimony of your declarations blooming to life over the past week.

3 **Discussion Questions:**
• Go around the room, saying one thing that you love about the person sitting to your right.

• No matter if you're single or married, you were created for intimacy and transparency within relationships. Do you have a hard time letting people see all of you?

• Do you believe you're worthy of love? Is it hard or easy for you to receive love?

• Sex and love are not the same things. Talk about what you believe, what the world portrays, and what God intended sex to be.

• When Studhubs saw me doing the thing I was the most ashamed of and loved me anyway, what was your reaction? Do you believe God sees and loves you as you are?

• Your heart is the most precious possession you have, and out of it flows life. Do you give it away easily or understand its worth?

• How hard was it to stand in front of the mirror and tell yourself what you love about yourself?

• What happened when you did?

4 **Close with a prayer, asking God to love you in the places you believe are unlovable.**

5 **Have _Chapter 9_ and the assignments completed by the next time you meet. (Pages 182-199)**

week nine
Chapter 9 The Destination

Day 1: **Progress Check**

Read pages 185-187 in Chapter 9.

I remember the day I stood on the bow of that Alaskan Cruise liner and wrote the intro to the final chapter of *God Loves Ugly*. Having been a touring musician for the entirety of my professional life, I had no idea what I was doing as an author and looked at my new endeavor as more of a hobby than anything to be taken seriously. I just knew how much I ached to see people find freedom, and words kept bubbling up from the inside of my heart, begging to be laid out on paper.

I wasn't on that Alaskan cruise for vacation—I was actually there working. The artist that I had toured with for years, Michael W. Smith, had filled a massive boat with Smitty fans, and we were there as his band to play concerts during the voyage. Michael had also invited author and pastor Max Lucado, who had brought his entire family along with him.

In my down time on that cruise, I'd retreat to my cabin to write, hoping to finish the book I had started but had no idea how to end—or what to do with it when I did. But on that particularly chilly day as we cruised through icy blue waters, I felt like I was supposed to take my manuscript and go work up on the Lido deck of the ship. And that's when I ran into the Lucado clan.

"Whatcha got there, Christa?" Max's wife Denalyn Lucado peered down at my arms folded tightly around an unfinished manuscript.

"Oh, it's just a book I've been writing," I responded, a little embarrassed. I was confident in my ability as a musician, but not so much as an author. Especially as an author talking to the wife of an international best selling author.

"Oh, really?" she responded with a smile. "Well my daughter Andrea here is an editor for a publishing company, and she's really good. You guys should talk!"

And just like that, all the puzzle pieces began to come together to get *God Loves Ugly* where God wanted it all along—in your hands.

It wasn't by mistake you picked up this book. It wasn't by mistake you went on this journey with me. There are dry places in all of our hearts where Father leads us to water, and hopefully after the last eight weeks, your heart feels like it's been led to an oasis that never goes dry.

Can you see the fingerprints of God leading you towards freedom? Take a few moments and encourage your heart, acknowledging how Father worked and acted to lead you to deeper freedom in the past days and weeks.

_____

_____

_____

_____

There's nothing that encourages me in the present like remembering what God has already done for me. In fact, the only time I like to recall the past is to remember all that Father has done—otherwise, living in the past means living in a realm that can never be changed. But reminding yourself of all God has done brings hope to your present situation.

In Psalm 77, the psalmist isn't in a very good place emotionally, probably because his circumstances aren't so great. He tells us about his plight in verses 1-10:

I yell out to my God, I yell with all my might,
I yell at the top of my lungs. He listens.
I found myself in trouble and went looking for my Lord;
my life was an open wound that wouldn't heal.
When friends said, "Everything will turn out all right,"
I didn't believe a word they said.
I remember God—and shake my head.
I bow my head—then wring my hands.
I'm awake all night—not a wink of sleep;
I can't even say what's bothering me.
I go over the days one by one,
I ponder the years gone by.
I strum my lute all through the night,
wondering how to get my life together.
Will the Lord walk off and leave us for good?
Will he never smile again?
Is his love worn threadbare?
Has his salvation promise burned out?
Has God forgotten his manners?
Has he angrily stalked off and left us?
"Just my luck," I said. "The High God goes out of business
just the moment I need him." (MSG)

Have you ever been in this frustrated emotional state? How often do you feel like this? Do you still feel like sometimes God leaves you out in the cold, going out of business the moment you need Him?

_____

_____

_____

What was the psalmist's solution for his despair? How did he get his heart out of the depths of hopelessness, and onto the vision of possibility and hope?

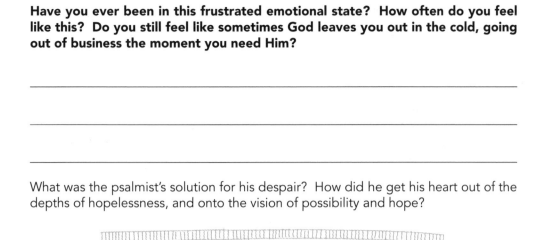

O God! Your way is holy!
No god is great like God!
You're the God who makes things happen;
you showed everyone what you can do—
You pulled your people out of the worst kind of trouble,
rescued the children of Jacob and Joseph.

Ocean saw you in action, God,
saw you and trembled with fear;
Deep Ocean was scared to death.
Clouds belched buckets of rain,
Sky exploded with thunder,
your arrows flashing this way and that.
From Whirlwind came your thundering voice,
Lightning exposed the world,
Earth reeled and rocked.
You strode right through Ocean,
walked straight through roaring Ocean,
but nobody saw you come or go.

Hidden in the hands of Moses and Aaron,
You led your people like a flock of sheep.

Psalm 77:11-15 (MSG)

The psalmist reminded himself of who God is, what God had done, and began to look at the solution instead of the problem.

He began to look at all God had done right, as opposed to all that was going wrong.

Hopefully in the last eight weeks, you've uncovered problems in your heart for the sole purpose of changing your focus.

For every lie you've believed, there is a promise that is greater.
For every hurt you've endured, there is a Healer who is stronger.

Take several minutes and track your progress, remembering where you were eight weeks ago. How has your life changed? How has your perspective changed? What has God done in your life? What are specifics, details, and stories that come to mind? Write them below.

_____

_____

_____

_____

_____

_____

_____

_____

_____

_____

Now that your vision is filled with all God has done, how does your heart feel?

_____

_____

_____

It sure is hard to be completely hopeless when you remember who God is and all He's done in your life.

Friend, you might not be exactly where you want to be. You might still have days where you battle food, addiction, fear, insecurity, anger, jealousy, sex, and bitterness. There will be moments where you do things that you do not want to do.

And when you start to look at all that's still wrong, you must stop and remember all that God has done right.

Take a few minutes and simply look up. Physically take your head and your eyes and look at the heavens. Look at the ceiling. Look at how limitless the sky is. Meditate on the God who is bigger than all your circumstances. Meditate on the God who only deals in abundance and solutions. Bathe in His goodness until His goodness is all that you see.

If you're anything like me, you need to have a plan of attack when the storms of life come. And that's why I created REM(MY) cards. For every promise God has made you, you need to remind yourself of that promise until it sticks. For every word of truth God is speaking over you, you need something in your face when the world is screaming the opposite.

REM(MY) means= Remind Myself

Each card has a reminder of the truth, and a place for you to write out the truth God has spoken to your heart. The more you see it, the more you speak it, and the more you begin to live it.

Check out the REM(MY) card set available at www.christablack.com

Day 2: Trials

Read 'Trials' on pages 187-190, and the first 'Your Turn' question on page 196.

I used to think that the fires and trials of life would cool down after I'd walked through enough heat. But I now understand, fire never dies down in a world filled with sin and death.

I just learned that I'm fireproof when the fire rages.

> *But now you have arrived at your destination: By faith in Christ you are in direct relationship with God. Your baptism in Christ was not just washing you up for a fresh start. It also involved dressing you in an adult faith wardrobe—Christ's life, the fulfillment of God's original promise.*
> *Galatians 5:26-29* (MSG)

Take a moment and meditate on the fact that you're dressed up in the perfect wardrobe—you're clothed with Jesus. You're in the safest place you could possibly ever be—you're *inside* of Jesus.

You've got the most incredible fireproof suit ever assembled because you're inside *the guy who conquered the flames.*

Close your eyes for a few minutes and see yourself inside this Jesus suit. What does it feel like to be clothed in Christ, in His victory, His promises, and His eternity? Write your experience below, explaining the feelings and thoughts you have being clothed with Christ.

_____

_____

_____

Did trials come against Jesus? You better believe they did. He was persecuted, rejected, scorned, falsely accused, betrayed, whipped, flogged, and crucified. *But not at the hand of the Father.* Friend, mankind did all these things to our Christ—God didn't do them. The Trinity had a plan to rescue us through the actions of man, but God didn't coerce or influence the Pharisees and Jewish people to bring accusation against the Savior of the world, leading to His death. They made those choices all on their own—and God knew they would choose death before the beginning of time. We live in a world where terrible things happen all the time because of the terrible choices of mankind, and until Jesus comes back, bad choices will continue to be made.

Which means, if trials are inevitable in this world, instead of trying to avoid them, shouldn't we find out how to have peace in the midst of them?

Maybe you've run from trials, like I explained on page 187. Do you avoid pain at all cost? What stance do you take when storms come against your life? Have you been someone who runs from conflict? Write down your approach to trials in the space below.

_____

_____

_____

"The problem with this approach (running from) the fire is this: You might not have learned everything you needed to learn in the midst of the trial, which means you will probably have to go through it again." -page 187 in *God Loves Ugly*

Think about your track record with trials. Are you constantly plagued with rejection? Maybe you're accident-prone. Do you always find yourself robbed or betrayed? Are you always the victim and not the victor? What patterns or consistencies do you see? Write them below.

_____

_____

_____

_____

_____

When I looked back at my life, rejection was my most common theme. Because I'd been so rejected, I expected people to reject me. My belief in myself wasn't in alignment with the promises of God—my belief was in alignment with the pain of my experiences. And because I expected to be rejected, I acted rejected, and then was rejected.

When I finally stopped trying to avoid rejection, turning around to face my pain, throwing my arms around it and embracing the suffering—then and only then did I learn what I needed to learn. I learned who I was. I learned who God was. And I learned who Jesus wanted me to become while being rejected so it wouldn't destroy me.

Let me tell you, I'm rejected way less than I used to be because I'm not living for people to love me anymore. I'm living to love people. And when they do throw their stones, it's just another opportunity within the flames for my heart to be purified so that I can give them what they need—unconditional love and forgiveness.

Is there suffering that you need to turn around and embrace? Have you been running from a relationship, a situation, confrontation, or pain that you need to turn around and confront head-on? Write down suffering that you might need to throw your arms around.

_____

_____

_____

Ask yourself this question right now, "What do I need to learn from this so I never have to go through it this way again?"

"All right, buddy—you're here, and I'm not running. What character can I take away from this pain? What strength can I glean from remaining still in the middle of a storm? What power can I obtain by learning how to stand in the heart of battle?"
-page 189, *God Loves Ugly*

Still your heart. Quiet your mind. And ask Father what He wants to show you about the situation. Ephesians 2 says you're seated in heavenly places, so look at the pain from His perspective. Write down what you discover and see.

_____

_____

_____

As you begin to see trials from heaven's perspective, the problem reduces in size because you're in relationship with the solution.

We might not like trials, but if we walk through them well, we like who we become.

What positives can you attribute to your past pain? What have you become that you like about yourself because of your trials? Have you become stronger, more forgiving, more loving, and wiser? List any positive attributes that grew inside of your heart because you went through something hard.

_____

_____

_____

Building a history with God is one of the most important things you could ever do. I'd never know the Comforter if I never had to be comforted. I'd never know the Healer if I never needed anything healed. I'd never known the Provider if I always had everything I needed. I'd never need the Lover of my soul if my soul always believed it was lovable. God isn't behind a lot of the storms that come at us, but He sure is good at redeeming them when they come. And in the process of walking through the mountains and valleys of life, holding hands with the most powerful person in the universe, an incredible thing happens.

Trust is built.

Certainty is assured.

And relationship is established.

Have you allowed the pain of life to help you build a history with God? Take a moment and write out your history of relationship with Him, chronicling the ups and downs, hurts and joys, laughs and tears.

_____

_____

_____

_____

_____

_____

_____

_____

Just like any relationship on this earth, your relationship with Father has to be cultivated. It takes time, effort, and intentionality. If you want to be committed to building a history and relationship with God through the ups and downs of life, write out a commitment to Him below.

I, _____, commit to this relationship—in good and bad, through highs and lows. I want to build a history with You, Father. I want to know Your character, Your whispers, and Your love more than anything else. I want You to teach me in the suffering, coaching me to turn around and face giants without fear. I want You to become bigger than my current struggle, which means, I simply need to keep looking at You.

Thank you, Father, for never giving up on our relationship. Thank you that your love is always coming at me from all sides as You long to win me to Your heart. I surrender to that love once again. Amen.

Day 3: **The Journey**

Read 'The Journey' on pages 190-193, and the Your Turn section on pages 197-199.

"The journey is the destination, Christa," he said softly. "The process you're in is the goal. Success is never defined by the outcome, but by the process."

-W. P. Young, author of *The Shack*

When you live in pain, it's almost impossible to live in the present moment. You can't. It's too painful. For most of my life, because my heart was in an outrageous amount of pain, I couldn't live in the moment, which kept me always looking towards the future, or shackled in the past.

But when the goal I had longed for was finally reached, and my heart was still in pain, I'd look up ahead at the future again; hoping something else would be my solution.

Have you struggled to live in the present moment? Are you always dissatisfied with your current situation, looking towards a relationship, achievement, a number in your bank account, a house, a jean size, or goal to finally make you feel happy and content? Write your answers below.

_____

_____

_____

Future tripping is a very dangerous thing. The only way I'm allowed to think, dream, and plan for the future is if I'm asking the Holy Spirit to show me, otherwise, I might just be imagining scenarios that will never, ever happen. When we play out in our imagination how our job loss will leave us evicted and on the street, we feel hopeless about something that might never happen. When we speculate why someone ignored us at church, playing out an entire suspicious scenario about how they must hate us, we feel insecure about something that might be explained away by realizing they're sick.

Like I said, thinking about the future without the Holy Spirit is dangerous, and it gets our hearts into all sorts of trouble.

Do you have a tendency to imagine scenarios about the future out of speculation or fear? Do you play out images of terrible things happening, or get angry or bitter at people because of a lack of information? Write any ways you future-trip without the Holy Spirit in the space below.

_____

_____

_____

While speaking at a Jesus Culture conference in Los Angeles, I sat around the table with a Super Bowl champion and an Olympic gold medalist. Both of them told the same story—once they became the best in the world, achieving life-long goals and dreams, one battled severe depression and the other sadness. The goal that they'd dreamed about their entire life had been reached, and a strange thing happened. It didn't make them happy. The gold medal and the Super Bowl ring didn't ensure life-long contentment. It didn't take away pain. It didn't fix their hearts. It didn't solve all their problems.

Have you looked towards a future goal and believed it will finally make you happy? Maybe you're waiting on your spouse, which is a hard thing to do while watching all of your friends get married and have kids. Maybe you believe you'll finally be happy if you reach a certain clothing size, or get a specific job. You might be waiting to feel contentment until you get a certain house, move to a certain city, or have a specific number in your bank account. Maybe you're longing to be free from cycles of addiction, or from physical pain and illness.

Write any ways you're dissatisfied with what you have right now, hoping for contentment when you get something in the future.

_____

_____

_____

What if you could find contentment right now? What if happiness was within your reach, even before you got what you thought would make you happy?

This, dear friends, is the kingdom of life that we live in. It's a kingdom of joy in the midst of all circumstances. It's a kingdom of peace as the storms rage. After many ups and downs in life, I've finally realized contentment doesn't come from my circumstance—it's a heart issue. And because the God of the universe lives inside my heart, I can have contentment in all circumstances.

> *"I know what it is to be in need, and I know what it is to have plenty. I have learned the secret of being content in any and every situation, whether well fed or hungry, whether living in plenty or in want. I can do all this through him who gives me strength." Philippians 4:12-13* (NIV)

Your contentment, happiness, and joy can't be contingent on circumstances that are far outside of your control. They must be contingent on the one who lives inside of you, walking you through every experience, holding your hand, wiping your tears, and carrying you when you're too weak to walk.

Take a moment and think about what's in your hands right now. Maybe it's your kids, your family, a roof over your head, or food on the table. You have air to breathe and clean water. You might not be the person you want to be, but you never will be, and that's okay. No one ever arrives to a place of perfection this side of heaven—but your heart can be filled with peace in every circumstance.

What treasure have you missed out on because you've been searching for the gold of another day? Are you missing out on your kids because you're constantly escaping through the unrealistic facade of Facebook and Instagram? Are you always angry with your spouse because you want them to change, and you think that will fix everything? Have you forgotten all you've been blessed with because you're focused on what you're lacking?

Read pages 197-199 in *God Loves Ugly* and answer the questions below, listing the treasures you already have.

_____

_____

_____

_____

_____

_____

_____

Thank you, Father, that You've already given me so much. I repent for believing that happiness comes from an outcome, a circumstance, or a goal. I can be content in all circumstances because contentment is a heart issue—and You're living in my heart. I yield my heart to You, once again, committing to celebrate what's already in my hand. Amen.

Day 4: Treasure Hunters

> *"Do not lay up for yourselves treasures*
> *on earth, where moth and rust consume*
> *and where thieves break in and steal, but*
> *lay up for yourselves treasures in*
> *heaven, where neither moth nor rust*
> *consumes and where thieves do not break*
> *in and steal. For where your treasure is,*
> *there will your heart be also.*
> *Matthew 6:19-21*

Treasure on this earth isn't what I once believed. Of course, I still want physical things while still breathing on this planet, and there's nothing wrong with that. I dream about my future house, especially since I've been living out of suitcases for years while traveling the world. And I'll always enjoy the amenities of living in our Western culture, loving my hot baths, toilet paper, and long massages.

But those things aren't the source of my happiness anymore. They're blessings on top of a heart that contends to remain in my inheritance of peace.

Where is your treasure? Do you treasure your possessions, your looks, your job, or material things? If you want to know what is most valuable to you, look at where you spend the most time. Is it your body, is it work, is it eating, a computer or smartphone, or maybe relationships? Write down your greatest treasures in the chest below.

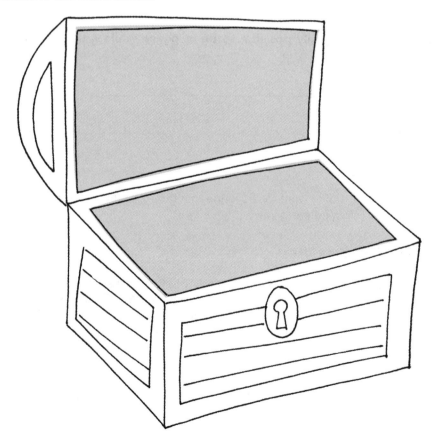

This morning, I looked down at my son Moses as he played cars. I simply stopped and watched him, enjoying every moment as he made little car sounds. Reality is, we're living out of suitcases, our stuff has been in storage for eleven months, and we're gone for an entire month while I travel and speak. On paper our life is chaos, we have no direction as to where we're supposed to live permanently, and no idea how to get there. But if I focused on all the things we don't have, I would most definitely be so overwhelmed that I wouldn't be able to enjoy the treasure that my son is *right now*. So in the midst of the whirlwind, I remind myself to take long sighs, drinking deeply of each moment, sit down on the floor, and play cars every once in a while.

Stop. What can you stop and enjoy in this moment that you might have been missing? Take a minute and breathe deeply, being fully present within each second.

_____

_____

_____

What is a stressful situation that you're currently in, or have been in recently? What constantly stresses you out?

_____

_____

_____

Do you think it's physically possible to be at peace while going through that situation?

_____

_____

_____

If your answer is 'no,' then I want to challenge that thought. If your answer is 'yes, but I don't know how,' then let me give you the answer.

Gratitude brings freedom.

It really is that simple. The more you cultivate gratitude in everything you go through, the easier it is to go through hard situations. Find treasure in the storms. Look at the positives instead of the negatives. Focus on how far you've come instead of how far you still have to go. Be grateful in the famine and in the harvest.

Now, I want you to test this theory.

The next time you get around the person who annoys you the most, or right after you fail miserably with an addiction—the moment you burn your dinner, and all the kids are screaming for no reason—STOP. Take a deep breath. Find something to be grateful for. Find the treasure. Remember, you're not at the end of your life; you're in the middle of your story. Focus on something that you have, rather than all you don't— and let gratitude begin to bloom deep inside your soul.

After testing this theory, write the outcome below. (And if you had a hard time finding treasure, try it again and again until you do! Remember, treasure is a heart issue, not an outcome!)

_____

_____

_____

_____

_____

_____

_____

Day 5: And In Conclusion

Dear friend, you've done it. You've committed to letting God love the ugly parts of your life, and found that His love really does bring beauty from the ashes, life from the death, and healing from the pain.

Check all boxes that apply below:

☐ **You've committed to uncover the lies, replacing them with the truth.**

☐ **You've committed to challenge the word daggers, replacing them with words of life.**

☐ **You've committed to uncover the roots behind your emotions and behaviors, finding healing so you can change from the inside out.**

☐ **You've committed to pulling back the veil from your heart and let Love go deep inside—pouring in love that casts out all fear.**

☐ **You've committed to look for treasure in all circumstances, guarding your heart with peace and contentment.**

And now, you get the beautiful privilege of walking this newness out, holding hands with the safest, most loving, most powerful person in the universe.

The Holy Spirit loves for you to dream with Him, and He has more for you than you could possibly imagine.

> *"Now to him who by the power at work*
> *within us is able to do far more abundantly*
> *than all that we ask or think, to him be*
> *glory in the church and in Christ Jesus to*
> *all generations, for ever and*
> *ever. Amen." Ephesians 3:20* (ESV)

Take a few minutes and ask the Holy Spirit to rise up in you, leading you into all truth. Ask Him what plans He has for your future (Jeremiah 29:11). Ask Him what treasures He's cultivating inside your heart. Ask Him what 'exceedingly, abundantly' looks like, and begin to imagine it in your life. Ask Him specifics, ask Him for dreams, and ask Him for visions.

Write what you hear, see, and experience below.

_____

_____

_____

_____

_____

_____

_____

You're in relationship with a good God who has good things for you—who has never left you or forsaken you. (Deuteronomy 31:6) And as this last chapter closes, newness of life begins, because that's how He works.

"And I am sure that he who began
a good work in you will bring it to completion
at the day of Jesus Christ." Philippians 1:6

Commit to walking this road of healing with Him for the rest of your life. Commit to surrendering to Him when you're weak, letting Him carry you through darkness. Commit to the journey, knowing every moment is the destination.

I, _____, commit to this road, knowing I am never alone. I commit to lay my head against Your heart and hear how it beats with love for me. I commit to receiving so I have an abundance to give. I commit to looking at Your face instead of my problems. And I commit to the wholeness of my heart—knowing You're the solution for every problem I will ever face.

I love you Jesus. I love You with all my heart. Amen.

Week 9: GROUP DISCUSSION QUESTIONS

Chapter 9, The Destination

1 **Begin with a prayer, thanking God for life, and life abundantly! (John 10:10)**

2 **Read the 'We Believe God Can' list aloud.** Take a moment to thank Him for the things on your list that have happened! Briefly give any testimony of your declarations blooming to life over the past week.

3 **Discussion Questions:**
• You're almost finished! Talk about the changes that have happened in your thinking, your emotions, and your behaviors over the last nine weeks.

• The journey is the destination. Are you able to have grace for yourself today, wherever you are in the journey? Can you find joy in any circumstance?

• Gratitude brings freedom. What are some ways you can practice gratitude in your life? How does this change your perspective?

• What has God brought to the surface during this study that He's removing?

• What trials are you learning to turn around and face that you used to run from? How do you feel about yourself when you face your fears?

• Take a moment and tell the group how contending for freedom in your own life has changed your family, your friends, and your relationships.

• What is one thing you're taking away from this study that you're going to practice for the rest of your life? What has changed you more than anything else?

• Commit to praying and supporting one another on the journey of walking out wholeness.

4 **Close with a prayer, thanking God that He will continue the good work that He began, carrying it to completion. (Philippians 1:6)**

ABOUT CHRISTA

It's hard to put just one label on Christa Black.

She's a multi-platinum selling songwriter and her hit song **One Thing Remains** went number #1 in both 2012 and 2013. She's a profession musician who toured for over a decade, sharing the stage with renowned artists **The Jonas Brothers, Michael W. Smith, Jordin Sparks,** and **Israel Houghton.** She's a dynamic worldwide speaker and was a keynote for **Women of Faith's Revolve Tour** alongside Natalie Grant, Christine Caine, and Brit Nicole. She's a popular blog writer nearing 1 million page views, and a writer for **The Huffington Post** where her blog *Embracing The Pain of Losing a Child* was featured in **Best of Huffington Post.** Her first book **God Loves Ugly** was birthed out of a blog while on tour with the Jonas Brothers in 2009. She would climb on the tour bus each night after the concert and teach her audience—who just happened to be over 3 million girls—how to walk into freedom from eating disorders, cutting, self-hatred, insecurity, depression, and addiction.

Christa found out very quickly that her Jonas Brother audiences weren't the only ones in pain— or the only ones reading her words. Messages from mothers, fathers, grandmothers, and brothers began to fill her email inbox, spilling their testimonies of finding freedom after applying her practical words to the pain in their lives.

As a former addict, rehab patient, and someone who has overcome sexual abuse, deep rejection, and found true healing from the agony of losing a child, Christa lives her life to lead those who are stuck in cycles of pain into a place she knows well: a reality called freedom, peace, and joy. Her life-goal is to provide resources for those broken by the pain of life, leading them into wholeness of the heart.

She's married to the love of her life, Lucas Gifford, and has a son, Moses Grae Lionheart, and a daughter in heaven, Luca Gold.